# TEACHER'S PET PUBLICATIONS

LITPLAN TEACHER PACK
for
The Red Pony
based on the book by
John Steinbeck

Written by
Mary B. Collins

© 1996 Teacher's Pet Publications
All Rights Reserved

This **LitPlan** for John Steinbeck's
The Red Pony
has been brought to you by Teacher's Pet Publications, Inc.

Copyright Teacher's Pet Publications 1996
11504 Hammock Point
Berlin MD 21811

Only the student materials in this unit plan (such as worksheets, study questions, and tests) may be reproduced multiple times for use in the purchaser's classroom.

For any additional copyright questions,
contact Teacher's Pet Publications.

www.tpet.com

TABLE OF CONTENTS - *The Red Pony*

Introduction	5
Unit Objectives	8
Reading Assignment Sheet	9
Unit Outline	10
Study Questions (Short Answer)	13
Quiz/Study Questions (Multiple Choice)	19
Pre-reading Vocabulary Worksheets	31
Lesson One (Introductory Lesson)	43
Nonfiction Assignment Sheet	46
Oral Reading Evaluation Form	48
Writing Assignment 1	45
Writing Assignment 2	54
Writing Assignment 3	59
Writing Evaluation Form	60
Vocabulary Review Activities	57
Extra Writing Assignments/Discussion ?s	56
Unit Review Activities	62
Unit Tests	65
Unit Resource Materials	95
Vocabulary Resource Materials	111

A FEW NOTES ABOUT THE AUTHOR
JOHN STEINBECK

STEINBECK, John (1902-68). Winner of the 1962 Nobel prize for literature, the American author John Steinbeck is best remembered for his novel 'The Grapes of Wrath'. Steinbeck's story of a family of farm workers migrating from Oklahoma to California describes the hopelessness of the Great Depression era.

John Ernst Steinbeck was born on Feb. 27, 1902, in Salinas, Calif. He took classes at Stanford University for several years but left without a degree. He worked as a laborer to support himself while he wrote. Steinbeck's first novel was published in 1929, but it was not until the publication of 'Tortilla Flat' in 1935 that he attained critical and popular acclaim.

He followed this success with 'In Dubious Battle' (1936) and 'Of Mice and Men' (1937). 'The Grapes of Wrath' (1939) earned for Steinbeck a Pulitzer prize. In these works Steinbeck's proletarian themes are expressed through his portrayal of the inarticulate, dispossessed laborers who populate his American landscape. Both 'Of Mice and Men' and 'The Grapes of Wrath' were made into motion pictures.

In 1943 Steinbeck traveled to North Africa and Italy as a war correspondent. Some of his later works include 'Cannery Row' (1945), 'The Red Pony' (1947), 'East of Eden' (1952), 'The Winter of Our Discontent' (1961), and 'Travels with Charley' (1962). He also wrote several motion-picture scripts, including adaptations of two of his shorter works-'The Pearl' and 'The Red Pony'. Steinbeck died in New York City on Dec. 20, 1968.

--- Courtesy of Compton's Learning Company

INTRODUCTION - *The Red Pony*

This unit has been designed to develop students' reading, writing, thinking, and language skills through exercises and activities related to *The Red Pony* by John Steinbeck. It includes sixteen lessons, supported by extra resource materials.

The **introductory lesson** introduces students to one main theme of the novel through a writing assignment. Following the introductory activity, students are given a transition to explain how the activity relates to the book they are about to read. Following the transition, students are given the materials they will be using during the unit. At the end of the lesson, students begin the pre-reading work for the first reading assignment.

The **reading assignments** are approximately thirty pages each; some are a little shorter while others are a little longer. Students have approximately 15 minutes of pre-reading work to do prior to each reading assignment. This pre-reading work involves reviewing the study questions for the assignment and doing some vocabulary work for 8 to 10 vocabulary words they will encounter in their reading.

The **study guide questions** are fact-based questions; students can find the answers to these questions right in the text. These questions come in two formats: short answer required or multiple choice-matching-true/false. The best use of these materials is probably to use the short answer version of the questions as study guides for students (since answers will be more complete), and to use the multiple choice version for occasional quizzes. It might be a good idea to make transparencies of your answer keys for the overhead projector.

The **vocabulary work** is intended to enrich students' vocabularies as well as to aid in the students' understanding of the book. Prior to each reading assignment, students will complete a two-part worksheet for approximately 8 to 10 vocabulary words in the upcoming reading assignment. Part I focuses on students' use of general knowledge and contextual clues by giving the sentence in which the word appears in the text. Students are then to write down what they think the words mean based on the words' usage. Part II nails down the definitions of the words by giving students dictionary definitions of the words and having students match the words to the correct definitions based on the words' contextual usage. Students should then have an understanding of the words when they meet them in the text.

After each reading assignment, students will go back and formulate answers for the study guide questions. Discussion of these questions serves as a **review** of the most important events and ideas presented in the reading assignments.

After students complete reading the work, a lesson is devoted to the **extra discussion questions/writing assignments**. These questions focus on interpretation, critical analysis and personal response, employing a variety of thinking skills and adding to the students' understanding of the novel.

Following the discussion session, there is a **vocabulary review** lesson which pulls together all of the fragmented vocabulary lists for the reading assignments and gives students a review of all of the words they have studied.

There is a **group unit project**. Students are divided into four groups: gifts, mountains, promises, and leaders. Each group researches its topic and prepares a fifteen minute presentation.

There is a **group activity** which has students working in small groups to discuss the main themes of the novel. Using the information they have acquired so far through individual work and class discussions, students get together to further examine the text and to brainstorm ideas relating to the themes of the novel.

The group activity is followed by a **reports and discussion** session in which the groups share their ideas about the themes with the entire class; thus, the entire class is exposed to information about all of the themes and the entire class can discuss each theme based on the nucleus of information brought forth by each of the groups.

There are three **writing assignments** in this unit, each with the purpose of informing, persuading, or having students express personal opinions. The first assignment is to express personal opinions: students write a composition in which they tell about something they have wanted very much. The second assignment is to inform: students write a composition in which they explain what they will do for their group presentations. The third assignment is to persuade: students write a letter persuading someone to let them do something they want to do or let them have something they want to have.

There is a **nonfiction reading assignment**. Students are required to read a piece of nonfiction related in some way to *The Red Pony*. Most students will accomplish this while doing their group unit project. After reading their nonfiction pieces, students will fill out a worksheet on which they answer questions regarding facts, interpretation, criticism, and personal opinions. During one class period, students make **oral presentations** about the nonfiction pieces they have read. This not only exposes all students to a wealth of information, it also gives students the opportunity to practice **public speaking**.

The **review lesson** pulls together all of the aspects of the unit. The teacher is given four or five choices of activities or games to use which all serve the same basic function of reviewing all of the information presented in the unit.

The **unit test** comes in two formats: all multiple choice-matching-true/false or with a mixture of matching, short answer, multiple choice, and composition. As a convenience, two different tests for each format have been included.

There are additional **support materials** included with this unit. The **unit resource** section includes suggestions for an in-class library, crossword and word search puzzles related to the novel, and extra vocabulary worksheets. There is a list of **bulletin board ideas** which gives the teacher suggestions for bulletin boards to go along with this unit. In addition, there is a list of **extra class activities** the teacher could choose from to enhance the unit or as a substitution for an exercise the teacher might feel is inappropriate for his/her class. **Answer keys** are located directly after the **reproducible student materials** throughout the unit. The student materials may be reproduced for use in the teacher's classroom without infringement of copyrights. No other portion of this unit may be reproduced without the written consent of Teacher's Pet Publications, Inc.

UNIT OBJECTIVES - *The Red Pony*

1. Through reading John Steinbeck's *The Red Pony*, students will gain a better understanding of the "coming of age" theme as they are exposed to the main character's growth to maturity..

2. Students will demonstrate their understanding of the text on four levels: factual, interpretive, critical and personal.

3. Students will be exposed to a variety of ideas and information regarding gifts, mountains, promises, and leaders.

4. Students will be given the opportunity to practice reading aloud and silently to improve their skills in each area.

5. Students will answer questions to demonstrate their knowledge and understanding of the main events and characters in *The Red Pony* as they relate to the author's theme development.

6. Students will enrich their vocabularies and improve their understanding of the novel through the vocabulary lessons prepared for use in conjunction with the novel.

7. The writing assignments in this unit are geared to several purposes:
    a. To have students demonstrate their abilities to inform, to persuade, or to express their own personal ideas

    Note: Students will demonstrate ability to write effectively to <u>inform</u> by developing and organizing facts to convey information. Students will demonstrate the ability to write effectively to <u>persuade</u> by selecting and organizing relevant information, establishing an argumentative purpose, and by designing an appropriate strategy for an identified audience. Students will demonstrate the ability to write effectively to <u>express personal ideas</u> by selecting a form and its appropriate elements.

    b. To check the students' reading comprehension
    c. To make students think about the ideas presented by the novel
    d. To encourage logical thinking
    e. To provide an opportunity to practice good grammar and improve students' use of the English language.

8. Students will read aloud, report, and participate in large and small group discussions to improve their public speaking and personal interaction skills.

READING ASSIGNMENT SHEET - *The Red Pony*

Date Assigned	Reading Assignment	Completion Date
	The Gift	
	The Great Mountains	
	The Promise	
	The Leader of the People	

UNIT OUTLINE - *The Red Pony*

1 Introduction Writing Asst. 1 PV Gift	2 Read Gift	3 Study ?s Gift PVR Mountains	4 Study?s Mountains Group Project Assignment PVR Promise	5 Library
6 Study?s Promise Group Work	7 Writing Assignment 2 PVR Leader	8 Study ?s Leader Extra ?s	9 Vocabulary	10 Reports
11 Reports	12 Group Activity (Themes)	13 Reports & Discussion	14 Writing Assignment 3	15 Review
16 Test				

Key: P = Preview Study Questions   V = Vocabulary Work   R = Read

STUDY GUIDE QUESTIONS

SHORT ANSWER STUDY GUIDE QUESTIONS - *The Red Pony*

I. The Gift
1. Identify Billy Buck, Carl Tiflin, Jody Tiflin.
2. What did Mr. Tiflin and Bill do in Salinas?
3. What did Jody do on his way to school?
4. What chores did Mrs. Tiflin have to remind Jody to do?
5. What was the gift, the surprise Mr. Tiflin and Bill had for Jody?
6. What name did Jody give the red pony?
7. What was the reaction of the six boys to Jody now that he had a pony?
8. Why did Mrs. Tiflin feel "a curious pride rise up in her"?
9. How did Jody change after he got the pony?
10. Describe Billy's relationship with Jody.
11. How did Jody know the red pony was a good horse?
12. "Billy looked away. . . . He had no right to be fallible and he knew it." Explain.
13. What happened to the red pony?
14. What did Jody do to the buzzard? Why?
15. How did Mr. Tiflin react to Jody when he found him with the pony and buzzard? How did Billy react?

II. The Great Mountains
1. What kinds of things did Jody do at the beginning of this chapter?
2. Why were the mountains "dear to him, and terrible"?
3. Who visited the Tiflin farm and why did he come?
4. What was Mr. Tiflin's reaction to the man? Jody's?
5. Identify Easter.
6. In the conversation about Easter and the old man, what comparison did Mr. Tiflin make?
7. "Carl was afraid he might relent and let the old man stay, and so he continued to remind himself that this couldn't be." What do we learn about Mr. Tiflin's character through this passage? What kind of a man is he?
8. What happened to Gitano and Easter?

III. The Promise
1. In the spring, who marched home from school with Jody?
2. What did Jody do on the way home from school?
3. What deal does Jody make with his father?
4. How does the new responsibility affect Jody?
5. "And he [Billy] walked away from Jody and went into the saddle-room beside the barn, for his feelings were hurt." Why were his feelings hurt?

Red Pony Short Answer Study Questions Page 2

6. Where was Jody's special place, his "center-point"?
7. What place was "repulsive" to Jody?
8. What did Jody decide to name the colt?
9. What kinds of daydreams did Jody have about the colt?
10. What was "the promise"?
11. What happened to Nellie?
12. "He tried to be glad because of the colt, but the bloody face, and the haunted, tired eyes of Billy Buck hung in the air ahead of him." What do we learn about Jody from this passage?

IV. <u>The Leader of the People</u>
1. Who was The Leader of the People?
2. What's Mr. Tiflin's attitude towards Grandfather? Jody's? Billy's?
3. What is Jody looking forward to doing with Grandfather?
4. What does Grandfather overhear?
5. Why does Jody decide to kill the mice another day?
6. What does Grandfather mean when he says "Westering has died out of the people"?
7. What does Mrs. Tiflin realize about Jody when he asks for only one lemon?

ANSWER KEY: STUDY GUIDE QUESTIONS - *The Red Pony*

<u>I. The Gift</u>

1. Identify Billy Buck, Carl Tiflin, Jody Tiflin.
    Billy Buck is the ranch hand. Carl Tiflin owns the ranch and is Jody's father. Jody is the main character, a young boy growing up on a ranch.

2. What did Mr. Tiflin and Bill do in Salinas?
    They sold the old cows to the butcher and bought Jody a pony.

3. What did Jody do on his way to school?
    Jody did typically boyish things like picking up little rocks and throwing them at birds.

4. What chores did Mrs. Tiflin have to remind Jody to do?
    Jody had to fill the wood box and look for stray hen nests with eggs.

5. What was the gift, the surprise Mr. Tiflin and Bill had for Jody?
    The gift was a red pony colt.

6. What name did Jody give the red pony?
    He named the pony Gabilan Mountains.

7. What was the reaction of the six boys to Jody now that he had a pony?
    The boys had more admiration for Jody. He was better than they were because he had the pony.

8. Why did Mrs. Tiflin feel "a curious pride rise up in her"?
    Mrs. Tiflin felt pride because her little boy was growing up and taking the responsibility for his own pony.

9. How did Jody change after he got the pony?
    He rose promptly in the morning and did all of his chores without being told to do them. He acted more like an adult.

10. Describe Billy's relationship with Jody.
    Billy was a good friend and a father figure for Jody.

11. How did Jody know the red pony was a good horse?
    The pony resented training and "only a mean-souled horse does not resent training."

12. "Billy looked away. . . . He had no right to be fallible and he knew it." Explain.
    Billy made very few errors concerning the animals. Jody trusted him completely, admired and respected him. To Jody, Billy could do no wrong, and Billy knew Jody felt this way.

13. What happened to the red pony?
    The red pony died.

14. What did Jody do to the buzzard? Why?
    Jody beat the bird to death with a quartz rock because he was sad, angry and frustrated. He had to take his feelings out on something, and he couldn't beat up Billy.

15. How did Mr. Tiflin react to Jody when he found him with the pony and buzzard? How did Billy react?
    Carl Tiflin was not particularly understanding. He only dealt with the obvious fact that the buzzard didn't kill the pony. He missed the point. Billy was concerned with Jody's feelings and had picked him up to take him home.

II. The Great Mountains

1. What kinds of things did Jody do at the beginning of this chapter?
    Jody again did boyish things. He snapped the dog's nose in a trap, tried to kill a bird with a slingshot, kicked the dirt with his toes, and dissected a bird he shot.

2. Why were the mountains "dear to him, and terrible"?
    They were a mysterious place he thought he would like to see, and yet they also held the fear of the unknown.

3. Who visited the Tiflin farm and why did he come?
    An old man, Gitano, came back to his home-place to die.

4. What was Mr. Tiflin's reaction to the man? Jody's?
    Mr. Tiflin did not want the old man to stay. Jody wanted him to stay so Gitano could tell him about the mountains.

5. Identify Easter.
    Easter was Mr. Tiflin's old horse.

6. In the conversation about Easter and the old man, what comparison did Mr. Tiflin make?
    Mr. Tiflin said, "Old things ought to be put out of their misery."

7. "Carl was afraid he might relent and let the old man stay, and so he continued to remind himself that this couldn't be." What do we learn about Mr. Tiflin's character through this passage? What kind of a man is he?

    Mr. Tiflin was probably a more compassionate man than he would let himself show. He perhaps sees compassion as a weakness in a man.

8. What happened to Gitano and Easter?

    Gitano took Easter and rode off into the mountains; one presumes they will die there.

III. The Promise

1. In the spring, who marched home from school with Jody?

    A phantom army with great flags and swords marched with Jody.

2. What did Jody do on the way home from school?

    Jody gathered toads, lizards, a snake, some grasshoppers and a newt and put them in his lunch pail.

3. What deal does Jody make with his father?

    Jody agrees to take care of the mare and do extra chores if Mr. Tiflin will pay to have Nellie, the mare, bred.

4. How does the new responsibility affect Jody?

    Jody "went to his work with unprecedented seriousness."

5. "And he [Billy] walked away from Jody and went into the saddle-room beside the barn, for his feelings were hurt." Why were his feelings hurt?

    Billy's feelings were hurt because he knew that Jody didn't admire him as much as he had before the red pony died. He knew he had been infallible before that, and now he was capable of failure.

6. Where was Jody's special place, his "center-point"?

    Jody's "center point" was at the brush line behind the house where spring water ran into an old green tub. There was a "patch of perpetually green grass" there.

7. What place was "repulsive" to Jody?

    The black cypress tree where the pigs were slaughtered was repulsive to Jody.

8. What did Jody decide to name the colt?

    He decided to name the colt Black Demon.

9. What kinds of daydreams did Jody have about the colt?
   He daydreamed that riding Black Demon he was a hero, a larger-than-life character.

10. What was "the promise"?
    Billy promised Jody he would see that he got a good colt.

11. What happened to Nellie?
    Billy had to kill Nellie to get the colt.

12. "He tried to be glad because of the colt, but the bloody face, and the haunted, tired eyes of Billy Buck hung in the air ahead of him." What do we learn about Jody from this passage?
    Jody is starting to think about someone other than himself. Getting the colt is important to him, but now Billy's feelings are important, too.

IV. The Leader of the People

1. Who was The Leader of the People?
   Mrs. Tiflin's father was the leader.

2. What's Mr. Tiflin's attitude towards Grandfather? Jody's? Billy's?
   Mr. Tiflin is cold towards the grandfather. He doesn't want him there and doesn't even try to be polite. Billy doesn't particularly like the old man's company, but he at least tries to be polite. Jody likes the old man's stories and is really glad to have him there.

3. What is Jody looking forward to doing with Grandfather?
   Jody is looking forward to killing mice in the hay stack.

4. What does Grandfather overhear?
   Grandfather overhears Carl's true thoughts and feelings towards him, that he doesn't want to hear the stories over and over again.

5. Why does Jody decide to kill the mice another day?
   Jody decides to kill the mice another day because he knows grandfather is feeling low. Killing the mice wouldn't be fun anymore.

6. What does Grandfather mean when he says "Westering has died out of the people"?
   He thinks people don't have the interest or stamina of the old pioneering spirit anymore.

7. What does Mrs. Tiflin realize about Jody when he asks for only one lemon?
   She realizes that Jody has grown up a great deal. He thinks totally of grandfather's wants and not at all of his own.

MULTIPLE CHOICE STUDY GUIDE/QUIZ QUESTIONS - *The Red Pony*

Chapter I (The Gift)

1. What is the ranch hand's name?
    a. It is Ben Stetson.
    b. It is Gabe Cypress.
    c. It is Billy Buck.
    d. It is Gitano Morales.

2. True or False: Jody Tiflin owns the ranch.
    a. True
    b. False

3. Who is the main character?
    a. It is Carl Tiflin.
    b. It is Billy Beck.
    c. It is the red pony.
    d. It is Jody Tiflin.

4. What did Mr. Tiflin and Bill do in Salinas?
    a. They bought 50 acres of land adjacent to what they already owned.
    b. They sold the old cows to the butcher and bought a pony.
    c. They got drunk and visited a brothel.
    d. They saw a lawyer about making Jody the beneficiary of Mr. Tiflin's will.

5. What did Jody do on his way to school?
    a. He picked up little rocks and threw them at birds.
    b. He hid in the bushes and scared the girls who were walking to school.
    c. He caught and killed frogs.
    d. He carved his initials into a few of the trees.

6. What chores did Mrs. Tiflin have to remind Jody to do?
    a. She reminded him to chop wood and feed the horses.
    b. She reminded him to water the garden and bring the cows home from the pasture.
    c. She reminded him to fill the wood box and look for stray hen nests with eggs.
    d. She reminded him to bank the fire and sweep the kitchen floor.

7. True or False. Mr. Tiflin took Jody to town with him to pick out the red pony.
    a. True
    b. False

8. What name did Jody give the pony?
    a. He called it Monterey Red.
    b. He called it Billy.
    c. He called it Rusty.
    d. He called it Gabilan Mountains.

The Red Pony Multiple Choice Study Questions Page 2

9. True or False: Mrs. Tiflin was angry at Jody because he was spending so much time with the pony.
    a. True
    b. False

10. What was the reaction of the six boys to Jody now that he had a pony?
    a. They were jealous, so they ignored him.
    b. They were not particularly interested, because they all had their own ponies.
    c. They had more admiration, because having a pony made him better than they were.
    d. They all wanted to be his friend so that he would give them rides.

11. How did Jody change after he got the pony?
    a. He rose promptly in the morning and did all of his chores without being told to.
    b. He became obsessed with the pony and ignored his chores and schoolwork.
    c. He became moody and sullen.
    d. He let his school work go, and his grades dropped.

12. Describe Billy's relationship with Jody.
    a. Billy was distant and cool.
    b. Billy competed with Jody for Carl's attention.
    c. Billy was a good friend and a father figure.
    d. Billy was deferential to Jody because he was the boss's son.

13. True or False: Jody knew the red pony was a good horse because the pony resisted training and "only a mean-souled horse does not resent training."
    a. True
    b. False

14. True or False: Billy had made several previous errors concerning the animals. His most recent mistake made Jody lose respect completely.
    a. True
    b. False

15. What happened to the red pony?
    a. It died naturally.
    b. It ran off and Jody never saw it again.
    c. It recovered.
    d. Billy shot it.

The Red Pony Multiple Choice Study Questions Page 3

16. True or False: Jody beat the buzzard to death with a rock because he was sad, angry, and frustrated.
    a. True
    b. False

17. How did Mr. Tiflin react when he found Jody?
    a. He was very understanding.
    b. He was not particularly understanding.
    c. He cried.
    d. He beat Jody.

18. How did Billy react when he found Jody?
    a. He ridiculed Jody for being "soft, like a woman".
    b. He was concerned with Jody's feelings and picked him up to take him home.
    c. He beat Jody.
    d. He scolded Jody.

The Red Pony Multiple Choice Study Questions Page 4

<u>Chapter II (The Great Mountains)</u>
19. Which of the following did Jody not do at the beginning of this chapter?
    a. He snapped the dog's nose in a trap.
    b. He tried to kill a bird with a slingshot.
    c. He kicked the dirt with his toes.
    d. He ignored his chores and refused to bathe.

20. Who visited the Tiflin farm and why did he come?
    a. The school principal came because Jody was misbehaving.
    b. An old man, Gitano, came back to his home-place to die.
    c. Billy's cousin from the East came to visit for a few months.
    d. Billy's brother came to visit on his way to Los Angeles.

21. True or False: Jody thought of the mountains as "dear to him, and terrible."
    a. True
    b. False

22. What was Mr. Tiflin's reaction to the visitor?
    a. He wanted the visitor to stay.
    b. He didn't want the visitor to stay.

23. What was Jody's reaction to the visitor?
    a. He wanted the visitor to stay and tell him stories.
    b. He wanted the visitor to leave because he was jealous of the attention the visitor received.

24. Identify Easter.
    a. Easter was the ranch-hand who worked on the Tiflin ranch before Billy. He was born on Easter, and no one knew his real name.
    b. Easter was Jody's pet cat, who was ten years old.
    c. Easter was Mr. Tiflin's old horse.
    d. Easter was Jody's baby sister.

25. True or False: In the conversation about Easter and the old man, Mr. Tiflin said, "Old things ought to be put out of their misery."
    a. True
    b. False

The Red Pony Multiple Choice Study Questions Page 5

26. "Carl was afraid he might relent and let the old man stay, and so he continued to remind himself that this couldn't be." What do we learn about Mr. Tiflin's character through this passage? What kind of a man is he?
    a. He is more compassionate than he would let himself show.
    b. He is indecisive and weak.
    c. He is paranoid.
    d. He is self-centered.

27. What happened to Gitano and Easter?
    a. They were shot by a drunken ranch hand.
    b. The town doctor took them in.
    c. They went off into the mountains together.
    d. They stayed on the ranch with the Tiflins.

The Red Pony Multiple Choice Study Questions Page 6

Chapter III (The Promise)

28. In the spring, who marched home from school with Jody?
    a. The whole class did. He had invited them for lunch.
    b. A phantom army with great flags and swords did.
    c. His new girlfriend did.
    d. The teacher did. Jody had been misbehaving.

29. What did Jody do on the way home from school?
    a. He kicked at so many rocks and twigs that he wore a hole in the toe of his shoe.
    b. He picked wild flowers to make a bouquet for his mother.
    c. He detoured to the pond to go fishing.
    d. He gathered toads, lizards, a snake, some grasshoppers, and a newt and put them in his lunch pail.

30. What deal does Jody make with his father in order to have the mare bred?
    a. He must get straight As on his report card.
    b. He has to go to church without complaining for six months.
    c. He has to do extra chores.
    d. He has to sell his dog.

31. True or False: Jody was not able to keep his part of the bargain.
    a. True
    b. False

32. How did Billy feel about Jody's questions about the birth of the colt?
    a. He felt secure that Jody still had complete confidence in him.
    b. He felt hurt that Jody didn't admire him as much as before.
    c. He thought they were stupid.
    d. He hadn't realized just how little Jody had learned about farm life.

33. Where was Jody's special place, his "center-point"?
    a. It was in the loft of the barn.
    b. It was in his bedroom, the only place he couldn't be disturbed.
    c. It was on the highest branch of his favorite tree.
    d. It was the brush line behind the house where spring water ran into an old green tub. There was a "patch of perpetually green grass" there.

34. What place was "repulsive" to Jody?
    a. The black cypress tree where the pigs were slaughtered was repulsive.
    b. The town cemetery was repulsive.
    c. The place on the ranch where the red pony died was repulsive.
    d. The compost heap was repulsive.

The Red Pony Multiple Choice Study Questions Page 7

35. What did Jody decide to name the colt?
    a. Mountain Hawk
    b. Billy-Jo
    c. Black Demon
    d. Wild One

36. What kinds of daydreams did Jody have about the colt?
    a. He kept dreaming that the colt would die.
    b. He fantasized about being a larger-than-life hero.
    c. He dreamed that the colt was so wild even he couldn't ride it, and he never enjoyed having it.
    d. He thought about traveling the world, and charging people money to watch his "wonder horse" do tricks. In his daydreams he got very rich.

37. What was "the promise?"
    a. Billy promised Jody he would get a good colt.
    b. Jody promised his parents he would always do his schoolwork and chores first, before playing with the colt.
    c. Mr. Tiflin promised Jody a new saddle when the colt was three years old.
    d. Mrs. Tiflin promised to make Jody a special riding outfit after the colt was born.

38. True or False: Billy had to kill Nellie to get the colt.
    a. True
    b. False

39. What do we learn about Jody after the birth of the colt?
    a. He is still a self-centered, spoiled little boy who always puts himself first.
    b. He is starting to think about other people.
    c. He isn't very smart.
    d. He is odd.

The Red Pony Multiple Choice Study Questions Page 8

Chapter IV (The Leader of the People)

40. Who was the Leader of the People?
    a. It was the governor of California.
    b. It was the last remaining chief of the Salinas Indian tribe.
    c. It was Mrs. Tiflin's father.
    d. It was Jody's new name for Billy.

41. What is Mr. Tiflin's attitude towards Grandfather?
    a. He welcomed him and enjoyed his company.
    b. He refused to have him in the house.
    c. He was afraid of the older man, and tolerated him.
    d. He was cold and impolite.

42. What was Jody's attitude towards Grandfather?
    a. He is glad to have him.
    b. He resents sharing the attention of his parents.
    c. He thinks the old man is stupid and senile.
    d. He is angry because he has to give up his bed.

43. True or False: Billy doesn't particularly like the old man, but at least he tries to be polite.
    a. True
    b. False

44. What is Jody looking forward to doing with Grandfather?
    a. Grandfather will teach him Indian sign language.
    b. He wants Grandfather to come to school and tell stories to the class.
    c. He wants to have Grandfather help him kill mice in the haystack.
    d. Grandfather will help him train the colt.

45. True or False: Grandfather overhears Carl's true thoughts and feelings towards him.
    a. True
    b. False

46. True or False: Jody goes ahead with his original plans despite his grandfather's feelings.
    a. True
    b. False

The Red Pony Multiple Choice Study Questions Page 9

47. Which of the following statements expresses Grandpa's sentiments about people?
    a. "The pioneer spirit is alive in a brave new world."
    b. "Westering has died out of the people."
    c. "People aren't as good as they used to be."
    d. "Nobody cares."

48. What does Mrs. Tiflin realize about Jody when he asks for only one lemon?
    a. He is very depressed.
    b. His tastes are changing.
    c. He is acting more and more like his father.
    d. He is thinking of someone else instead of himself.

ANSWER KEY - MULTIPLE CHOICE STUDY/QUIZ QUESTIONS
The Red Pony

Chapter I	Chapter II	Chapter III	Chapter IV
1. C	19. D	28. B	40. C
2. B	20. B	29. D	41. D
3. D	21. A	30. C	42. A
4. B	22. B	31. B	43. A
5. A	23. A	32. B	44. C
6. C	24. C	33. D	45. A
7. B	25. A	34. A	46. B
8. D	26. A	35. C	47. B
9. B	27. C	36. B	48. D
10. C		37. A	
11. A		38. A	
12. C		39. B	
13. A			
14. B			
15. A			
16. A			
17. B			
18. B			

PREREADING VOCABULARY WORKSHEETS

VOCABULARY - *The Red Pony*

<u>Chapter I</u> Part I: Using Prior Knowledge and Contextual Clues

Below are the sentences in which the vocabulary words appear in the text. Read the sentence. Use any clues you can find in the sentence combined with your prior knowledge, and write what you think the underlined words mean on the lines provided.

1. His eyes were a <u>contemplative</u>, watery gray and the hair which protruded from under his Stetson hat was spiky and weathered.

   _____

2. Some animals had died in the <u>vicinity</u>.

   _____

3. Nearly all of his father's presents were given with reservations which <u>hampered</u> their value somewhat.

   _____

4. "It's just a show saddle," Billy Buck said <u>disparagingly.</u>

   _____

5. His ears pivoted about and his eyes turned red with fear and with general <u>rambunctiousness</u>.

   _____

6. And in the schoolyard---it was too awful to <u>contemplate</u>.

   _____

7. He <u>whetted</u> the shining blade a long time on a little carborundum stone.

   _____

Vocabulary - *The Red Pony* Chapter I Continued

8. Doubletree Mutt looked into the barn, his big tail waving provocatively, and Jody was so incensed at his health that he found a hard black clod on the floor and deliberately threw it.

_____

Part II: Determining the Meaning - Match the vocabulary words to their dictionary definitions.

___ 1. contemplative   A. sharpened
___ 2. vicinity   B. thoughtful; meditative
___ 3. hampered   C. boisterousness; disorderliness
___ 4. disparagingly   D. enraged
___ 5. rambunctiousness   E. locality; proximity; a neighborhood
___ 6. contemplate   F. prevented action or progress of ; impeded
___ 7. whetted   G. belittlingly; reducing in esteem
___ 8. incensed   H. consider thoughtfully; take seriously.

Vocabulary - *The Red Pony* Chapter II

Part I: Using Prior Knowledge and Contextual Clues

Below are the sentences in which the vocabulary words appear in the text. Read the sentence. Use any clues you can find in the sentence combined with your prior knowledge, and write what you think the underlined words mean on the lines provided.

1. In the humming heat of a midsummer afternoon the little boy Jody <u>listlessly</u> looked about the ranch for something to do.

    _____

2. His eyes narrowed, his mouth worked <u>strenuously</u>, for the first time that afternoon he was intent.

    _____

3. He didn't care about the bird or its life, but he knew what older people would say if they had seen him kill it; he was ashamed because of their <u>potential</u> opinion.

    _____

4 & 5. When the peaks were pink in the morning they invited him among them: and when the sun had gone over the edge in the evening and the mountains were a purple-like despair, then Jody was afraid of them; then they were so impersonal and <u>aloof</u> that their very <u>imperturbability</u> was a threat.

    _____

    _____

6. He turned <u>abruptly</u>, and ran into the house for help, and the screen door banged after him.

    _____

7. He looked secretly at Gitano, to see whether he noticed the <u>parallel</u>, but the big bony hands did not move, nor did the dark eyes turn from the horse.

    _____

8. The hilt was pierced and <u>intricately</u> carved.

    _____

Vocabulary - *The Red Pony* Chapter II Continued

Part II: Determining the Meaning - Match the vocabulary words to their dictionary definitions.

___ 1. listlessly
___ 2. strenuously
___ 3. potential
___ 4. aloof
___ 5. imperturbability

___ 6. abruptly
___ 7. parallel
___ 8. intricately

A. suddenly; curtly; brusquely
B. distant; indifferent; apart
C. complexly arranged elements
D. indifferently; unenthusiastically
E. a comparison indicating likeness or analogy; equal distance apart at all points
F. latent; possible but not yet realized
G. not capable of being upset or disturbed
H. energetically; vigorously active

Vocabulary - *The Red Pony* Chapter III

Part I: Using Prior Knowledge and Contextual Clues

Below are the sentences in which the vocabulary words appear in the text. Read the sentence. Use any clues you can find in the sentence combined with your prior knowledge, and write what you think the underlined words mean on the lines provided.

1. In a mid-afternoon of spring, the little boy Jody walked <u>martially</u> along the brush-lined road toward his home ranch.

___

2. Now Jody marched seemingly alone, with high-lifted knees and pounding feet; but behind him there was a <u>phantom</u> army with great flags and swords, silent but deadly.

___

3. With a gentle forefinger he stroked the throat and chest until the horny-toad relaxed, until its eyes closed and it lay <u>languorous</u> and asleep.

___

4. But he couldn't remember, and besides it was impossible to know what action might later be <u>construed</u> as a crime.

___

5. He dragged one foot to give an impression of great innocence and <u>nonchalance</u>.

___

6. Jody climbed to the top of the fence and hung his feet over and looked <u>paternally</u> down at the mare.

___

7. The bay mare Nellie quickly grew <u>complacent</u>.

___

Vocabulary - *The Red Pony* Chapter III Continued

8. He felt badly about his lost <u>prestige</u>, and so he said, meanly, "I'll do everything I know, but I won't promise anything."

_____

9. Where the water spilled over and sank into the ground there was a patch of <u>perpetually</u> green grass.

_____

10. As usual the water place <u>eliminated</u> time and distance.

_____

Part II: Determining the Meaning - Match the vocabulary words to their dictionary definitions.

   ___ 1. martially   A. renown; power to command admiration
   ___ 2. phantom   B. debonair lack of concern; indifference
   ___ 3. languorous   C. gotten rid of; to leave out of consideration
   ___ 4. construed   D. in a military or warlike manner
   ___ 5. nonchalance   E. continually; endlessly
   ___ 6. paternally   F. in a fatherly manner
   ___ 7. complacent   G. an image that appears only in the mind; ghost
   ___ 8. prestige   H. still; sluggish; listless
   ___ 9. perpetually   I. explained; interpreted
   ___ 10. eliminated   J. self-satisfied; contented to a fault

Vocabulary - *The Red Pony* Chapter IV

Part I: Using Prior Knowledge and Contextual Clues
 Below are the sentences in which the vocabulary words appear in the text. Read the sentence. Use any clues you can find in the sentence combined with your prior knowledge, and write what you think the underlined words mean on the lines provided.

1. Those plump, sleek, arrogant mice were doomed.

___

2. As Billy went back to his work he said ominously, "You'd better ask him anyway."

___

3. His father looked down at him contemptuously.

___

4. Directly below him, in an oak tree, a crow congress had convened.

___

5. The story droned on, speeded up for the attack, grew sad over the wounds, struck a dirge at the burials on the great plains.

___

6. A race of giants had lived then, fearless men, men of a staunchness unknown in this day.

___

7. They had been hunting gophers in the dark, and although the four cats were full of gopher meat, they sat in a semi-circle at the back door and mewed piteously for milk.

___

8. It was a terrible thing to him to retract a word, but to retract it in shame was infinitely worse.

___

Red Pony Vocabulary Chapter IV Continued

9. Jody turned <u>disconsolately</u> away, and walked down toward the old haystack.

_____

Part II: Determining the Meaning - Match the vocabulary words to their dictionary definitions.

    ___ 1. arrogant   A. to recant; to withdraw an accusation
    ___ 2. ominously   B. haughty; contemptuous; overbearing
    ___ 3. contemptuously   C. sorrowfully; dejectedly
    ___ 4. convened   D. made a low, dull monotonous sound
    ___ 5. droned   E. forebodingly; threateningly; menacingly
    ___ 6. staunchness   F. that which moves to sympathy
    ___ 7. piteously   G. assembled; came together in a body
    ___ 8. retract   H. steadfastness; resoluteness
    ___ 9. disconsolately   I. disdainfully; scornfully

ANSWER KEY - VOCABULARY
The Red Pony

Chapter I	Chapter II	Chapter III	Chapter IV
1. H	1. D	1. D	1. B
2. E	2. H	2. G	2. E
3. F	3. F	3. H	3. I
4. G	4. B	4. I	4. G
5. C	5. G	5. B	5. D
6. B	6. A	6. F	6. H
7. A	7. E	7. J	7. F
8. D	8. C	8. A	8. A
		9. E	9. C
		10. C	

DAILY LESSONS

LESSON ONE

Objectives
1. To introduce *The Red Pony* unit.
2. To distribute books and other related materials
3. To preview the study questions for The Gift
4. To familiarize students with the vocabulary for The Gift
5. To give students the opportunity to practice writing to express their own opinions
6. To give the teacher the opportunity to evaluate students' writing skills

Activity #1

Distribute Writing Assignment #1. Discuss the directions in detail and give students about 3/4 of your class period to work on it. Tell students when the assignments should be handed in for grading.

TRANSITION: Tell students that in the story they are about to read, there is something the main character really wants -- a horse of his own.

Activity #2

Distribute the materials students will use in this unit. Explain in detail how students are to use these materials.

Study Guides Students should read the study guide questions for each reading assignment prior to beginning the reading assignment to get a feeling for what events and ideas are important in the section they are about to read. After reading the section, students will (as a class or individually) answer the questions to review the important events and ideas from that section of the book. Students should keep the study guides as study materials for the unit test.

Vocabulary Prior to reading a reading assignment, students will do vocabulary work related to the section of the book they are about to read. Following the completion of the reading of the book, there will be a vocabulary review of all the words used in the vocabulary assignments. Students should keep their vocabulary work as study materials for the unit test.

Reading Assignment Sheet You need to fill in the reading assignment sheet to let students know by when their reading has to be completed. You can either write the assignment sheet up on a side blackboard or Bulletin board and leave it there for students to see each day, or you can "ditto" copies for each student to have. In either case, you should advise students to become very familiar with the reading assignments so they know what is expected of them.

<u>Extra Activities Center</u> The unit resource portion of this unit contains suggestions for an extra library of related books and articles in your classroom as well as crossword and word search puzzles. Make an extra activities center in your room where you will keep these materials for students to use. (Bring the books and articles in from the library and keep several copies of the puzzles on hand.) Explain to students that these materials are available for students to use when they finish reading assignments or other class work early.

<u>Nonfiction Assignment Sheet</u> Explain to students that they each are to read at least one non-fiction piece from the in-class library at some time during the unit. Students will fill out a nonfiction assignment sheet after completing the reading to help you evaluate their reading experiences and to help the students think about and evaluate their own reading experiences.

<u>Books</u> Each school has its own rules and regulations regarding student use of school books. Advise students of the procedures that are normal for your school.

<u>Activity #3</u>

Show students how to preview the study questions and do the vocabulary work for The Gift. Tell students the vocabulary work should be completed prior to your next class meeting.

WRITING ASSIGNMENT #1 - *The Red Pony*

PROMPT

At some point in our lives, most of us have a special something we *really want* more than anything else in the world. It could be an object we want to have, something we wish would happen, or perhaps something we wish we could do.

Sometimes when what we most want comes true, we are overjoyed. Oddly enough, sometimes we are disappointed; it didn't turn out to be as great or as fulfilling as we had hoped.

Your assignment is to write a composition in which you tell about something you really want(ed). If you actually got what you wanted, tell also about how you felt after you got it. If you have not yet obtained that precious thing you want, tell how you think you will feel after you get it.

PREWRITING

What is it you want(ed)? Jot down what *it* is. Write out some things that describe it. Jot down some reasons why you want(ed) it. If you have received it, jot down a few notes about how you felt after you got it. If you have not received it yet, jot down a few notes about how you think you will feel after you get it.

DRAFTING

Write a paragraph in which you introduce what it is you want(ed). One way to do this is to tell about how you discovered you wanted it in the first place.

In the body of your paper, write one paragraph in which you describe *it*. Write one paragraph in which you give your reasons for wanting it.

Write one concluding paragraph in which you tell how you felt after you got it (or how you think you will feel after you get it.)

NOTE: This is not the only possible organization for your composition. If what you want to say fits better organized differently, feel free to do so. Just make sure you have an introduction, a body and a conclusion to your composition.)

PROMPT

When you finish the rough draft of your paper, ask a student who sits near you to read it. After reading your rough draft, he/she should tell you what he/she liked best about your work, which parts were difficult to understand, and ways in which your work could be improved. Reread your paper considering your critic's comments, and make the corrections you think are necessary.

PROOFREADING

Do a final proofreading of your paper double-checking your grammar, spelling, organization, and the clarity of your ideas.

NONFICTION ASSIGNMENT SHEET - *The Red Pony*
(To be completed after reading the required nonfiction article)

Name _____ Date _____

Title of Nonfiction Read _____

Written By _____ Publication Date _____

I. Factual Summary: Write a short summary of the piece you read.

II. Vocabulary
    1. With which vocabulary words in the piece did you encounter some degree of difficulty?

    2. How did you resolve your lack of understanding with these words?

III. Interpretation: What was the main point the author wanted you to get from reading his work?

IV. Criticism
    1. With which points of the piece did you agree or find easy to accept? Why?

    2. With which points of the piece did you disagree or find difficult to believe? Why?

V. Personal Response: What do you think about this piece? OR How does this piece influence your ideas?

LESSON TWO

Objectives
1. To read The Gift
2. To give students practice reading orally
3. To evaluate students' oral reading

Activity

Have students read The Gift of *The Red Pony* out loud in class. You probably know the best way to get readers with your class; pick students at random, ask for volunteers, or use whatever method works best for your group. If you have not yet completed an oral reading evaluation for your students this marking period, this would be a good opportunity to do so. A form is included with this unit for your convenience.

If students do not complete reading The Gift in class, they should do so prior to your next class meeting.

LESSON THREE

Objectives
1. To review the main events and ideas from The Gift
2. To preview the study questions for The Great Mountains
3. To familiarize students with the vocabulary in The Great Mountains
4. To read The Great Mountains

Activity #1

Give students a few minutes to formulate answers for the study guide questions for The Gift, and then discuss the answers to the questions in detail. Write the answers on the board or overhead transparency so students can have the correct answers for study purposes. Note: It is a good practice in public speaking and leadership skills for individual students to take charge of leading the discussions of the study questions. Perhaps a different student could go to the front of the class and lead the discussion each day that the study questions are discussed during this unit. Of course, the teacher should guide the discussion when appropriate and be sure to fill in any gaps the students leave.

Activity #2

Give students about fifteen minutes to preview the study questions for The Great Mountains and to do the related vocabulary work.

Activity #3

Tell students to read The Great Mountains prior to your next class period. If there is time remaining in this period, students may begin reading silently.

ORAL READING EVALUATION - *The Red Pony*

Name _____ Class _____ Date _____

SKILL	EXCELLENT	GOOD	AVERAGE	FAIR	POOR
Fluency	5	4	3	2	1
Clarity	5	4	3	2	1
Audibility	5	4	3	2	1
Pronunciation	5	4	3	2	1
_____	5	4	3	2	1
_____	5	4	3	2	1

Total _____ Grade _____

Comments:

LESSON FOUR

Objectives
1. To review the main ideas and events from The Great Mountains
2. To assign the prereading and reading work for The Promise
3. To make the group project assignment
4. To give students the opportunity to work together in small groups
5. To broaden students' understanding of promises, gifts, leaders, and mountains

Activity #1
Give students a few minutes to formulate answers for the study guide questions for The Great Mountains, and then discuss the answers to the questions in detail. Write the answers on the board or overhead transparency so students can have the correct answers for study purposes.

Activity #2
Tell students that prior to Lesson Six (give students a day/date) they should have done the prereading and reading work for The Promise.

Activity #3
Divide your class into four groups. Distribute the Project Assignment Sheet. Discuss the directions in detail. Give students time to begin working on their projects. Students should use this time to brainstorm ideas about their topics, make a list of topics to be researched, and assign topic(s) to group members so that when they go to the library in the next class time, they will already know what to research.

LESSON FIVE

Objectives
To give students the opportunity to use the library's resources to find information for their projects.

Activity
Take students to your school's library/media center. Tell students that this is the only day they will have to gather materials and information related to their projects. Give students this class time to gather materials and information.

PROJECT ASSIGNMENT SHEET - *The Red Pony*

PROMPT

Each of the four chapters in *The Red Pony* is titled appropriately for the content of the chapter, and each chapter makes a point about the title word or phrase. In class discussions we will (have) discuss(ed) these ideas. Each of the chapter titles also deserves attention outside of (or perhaps extended from) the context of the novelette.

ASSIGNMENT

You have been divided into four groups: Gifts, Mountains, Promises, and Leaders of the People. Your assignment is to thoroughly explore your topic and create a fifteen-minute presentation about your topic to the class.

REQUIREMENTS
1. Each group must elect a leader.
2. Each group must produce a list showing what task(s) each member has to do and date(s) by which those task(s) must be done.
3. Each group must produce an outline of their proposed presentation

GETTING STARTED -- Here are some tips/ideas/suggestions for each group:

Gifts: The idea of giving gifts is probably as old as mankind. What can you find about the history of gift-giving? Gifts are a part of many cultures in the world -- explore gift-giving in various cultures, various countries around the world. Assign specific countries/continents/time periods to specific group members to research. Also, consider gift-giving itself. What exactly is a gift? Is a gift a gift if something is expected in return? When is a gift a bribe? When is it appropriate to give a gift in our country? When is it appropriate to accept or refuse/return a gift in our country? Why do people give gifts? What should one do after receiving a gift? What if you hate the gift someone gives you? What is the proper etiquette regarding gifts in our society? What has been written about gift-giving? Consider the idea of commercial exploitation or corruption of the pure and simple idea of gift-giving. How does one decide on the value of the gift to be given? We often hear, "It's the thought that counts." How many people really believe that? Have you ever given someone a little gift but received from that person a big gift? What do we do about that? These are just a few questions/ideas for you to explore. Feel free to think of more on your own.

Red Pony Project Assignment Page 2

Mountains: Mountains have long been inspirational to mankind. In many religions, the mountains are considered special places where one can go to be closer to god(s). They often symbolize the hopes and aspirations of mankind. Where are the great mountain ranges of the world? Who lives in the mountains? How do the mountains affect the people who live in/near them? How do mountains affect weather? What things have been written about mountains? There are lots of cliches about mountains, such as "Don't make a mountain out of a mole hill." In what other literature, music or art(s) do mountains appear, and in what context? How have mountains in our country affected exploration and development over the years? Mountains are often referred to as "majestic." Why? What feelings are inspired in people by mountains? Many people make a trip to the mountains in the fall of the year to see the colorful foliage. Why? These are just a few questions/ideas for you to explore. Feel free to think of more on your own.

Promises: It starts when we're really little with things like, "Do you promise to be a good little boy/girl now?" . . . "Yes, Mommy." And it goes on from there. We make promises to people almost every day, and people make promises to us. Some promises are spoken and some are implied. Perhaps you actually tell your parent(s) you promise to be home by eleven o'clock. On the other hand, you may just know that they will be expecting you by eleven o'clock because that has always been your curfew time. The latter is more of an implied promise. Your curfew is eleven o'clock, and you know it. You didn't say you *wouldn't* be home by eleven, so by going out you have assumed the responsibility of the promise of being home by eleven even though you haven't spoken the words. Some promises are very important -- like marriage vows or oaths taken in a courtroom. There are product guarantees -- promises that the product will perform as advertised or expected. Other kinds of promises are things like telling your friend(s) you will meet them at a certain time to do something, political campaign promises, and all kinds of contracts. We even make a promise to our employers when we take on a job: we agree (promise) to show up for work on time and to do the work the boss tells us to do. How many different kinds of promises can you think of? Are some promises more important than others? What happens when we break our promises? Is a big brother's breaking his promise to buy his little sister ice cream the same as a politician who promised to cut taxes but gets into office and raises them? Why? Explain how promises are tied in with truth, pride, self-respect, and all sorts of other personal traits. What happens when our word (our promise) isn't any good? Who are some people who have made famous promises throughout history? Were the promises kept or broken? What effect did it have? How are promises important to our society? These are just a few questions/ideas for you to explore. Feel free to think of more on your own.

Red Pony Project Assignment Page 3

Leaders of the People: What is a leader? What characteristics do leaders have? Who have been some great leaders of people throughout history? Brainstorm a list and tell a little about each person. What effect did they have? Are all politicians great leaders? Why or why not? Are all great leaders politicians? Explain why or why not and give examples. Who are the current leaders of the people in the world, our country, your state, your county/district, your city/town, and your school? Who are these people, and how did they become leaders? Be specific. Who have been some of the worst leaders of the people in history? Why do people follow leaders, and how do leaders manipulate people? These are just a few questions/ideas for you to explore. Feel free to think of more on your own.

A WORD ABOUT YOUR PRESENTATIONS

    Creative. That's the word about your presentations. Be creative; we all don't want to sit here and listen to a bunch of boring, dull, drab, ho-hum reports read from papers or index cards. Blah. Show some imagination in your presentations. Do things differently. Costumes, videos, humor, skits, or visuals (pictures, photos, overhead projections, maps, etc.) add so much to presentations. It takes extra time, sometimes a little expense, and always more effort, but putting together a creative presentation is well worth the investment. Everyone enjoys the presentation more and is more likely to remember the information presented, and you will have made something you can really be proud of. Do your best!

LESSON SIX

Objectives
1. To review the main ideas from The Promise
2. To give students time to work on their project assignments
3. To assign the prereading and reading work for The Leader of the People

Activity #1

Ask students to get out their books and some paper (not their study guides). Tell students to write down ten questions (and answers) which cover the main events and ideas from The Promise.

Discuss the students questions and answers orally, making a list of the questions with brief responses on the board. Put a star next to the students' questions and answers that are essentially the same as the study guide questions. (Be sure that all the study guide questions are answered.)

Activity #2

Tell students that prior to Lesson Eight (give students a day/date), they should have completed the prereading and reading work for The Leader of the People.

Activity #3

Give students this class time to work on their projects. Students should have gathered information about their topics. They should use this class time to read and share the information they have gathered so they know what material they will have to present.

LESSON SEVEN

Objectives
1. To help students prepare for their oral presentations
2. To give students the opportunity to practice writing to inform
3. To give the teacher the opportunity to evaluate students' writing and the progress of the group work

Activity

Distribute Writing Assignment #2. Discuss the directions in detail and give students ample time to complete the assignment. Tell students when the assignment should be handed in for grading.

WRITING ASSIGNMENT # 2 - *The Red Pony*

PROMPT

You have gathered information about your topic, and in a few days you will have to give an oral presentation about that information. The purpose of this assignment is to help you prepare for that presentation. Your assignment is to write a composition in which you explain what you plan to do in your presentation.

PREWRITING

Briefly review your information and jot down the different kinds of information you have to present. Next to each kind of information you have to present, jot down a few ideas as to how that information could be presented in an interesting and creative way. Keep in mind that you do *not* have to have a different way for presenting each kind of information you have. You *could* adopt an over-all scheme for the entire presentation and simply divide it into segments. For example, make the whole thing a play, and divide it into acts, or make the whole thing a news broadcast and divide it into individual roving reporter reports, or make the whole thing a comedy routine divided into segments. Decide on how you will present your material. Make an outline showing in what order (and how) your information will be presented.

Make a punch list of materials you will need, possible problems you may have and possible solutions to those problems.

Also remember that if you are doing skits, reports, a humorous routine, or other device, the script(s) for what you will actually say and do will have to be written. This writing assignment only gets your plan set up. Next you will have to do the actual writing of your presentation.

DRAFTING

Write a paragraph in which you introduce your topic and give an overview of the general format of your presentation.

In the body of your composition, write one paragraph for each segment of your presentation. Each paragraph should give the details of what the segment will include, who will be doing the presenting, and how that segment will be presented.

Write a concluding paragraph in which you tell about possible problems you may have and offer possible solutions to those problems should they occur.

Along with your composition, you must also have a list of specific tasks each group member is to perform and dates by which those tasks have to be completed.

PROOFREADING

Several group members should proofread the composition prior to handing it in. Make any necessary corrections.

LESSON EIGHT

Objectives
1. To review the main ideas and events from The Leader of the People
2. To discuss *The Red Pony* on interpretive and critical levels

Activity #1
Take a few minutes at the beginning of the period to review the study questions for The Leader of the People.

Activity #2
Choose the questions from the Extra Discussion Questions/Writing Assignments which seem most appropriate for your students. A class discussion of these questions is most effective if students have been given the opportunity to formulate answers to the questions prior to the discussion. To this end, you may either have all the students formulate answers to all the questions, divide your class into groups and assign one or more questions to each group, or you could assign one question to each student in your class. The option you choose will make a difference in the amount of class time needed for this activity.

Activity #3
After students have had ample time to formulate answers to the questions, begin your class discussion of the questions and the ideas presented by the questions. Be sure students take notes during the discussion so they have information to study for the unit test.

LESSON NINE

Objective
To review all of the vocabulary work done in this unit

Activity
Choose one (or more) of the vocabulary review activities listed after the extra discussion questions and spend your class period as directed in the activity. Some of the materials for these review activities are located in the vocabulary resource section of this unit.

EXTRA WRITING ASSIGNMENTS/DISCUSSION QUESTIONS - *The Red Pony*

Interpretation

1. What point of view does Steinbeck use for *The Red Pony*? How does this contribute to our understanding of the themes in the story?
2. Write a list of the main events in *The Red Pony*.
3. Is the story of *The Red Pony* believable? Why or why not?
4. What are the main settings throughout the story? What do they add to the story?
5. Are the characters in *The Red Pony* stereotypes? If so, why are stereotypes used? If not, explain how they merit individuality?
6. What are the main conflicts in the story, and how are they resolved?
7. Where is the climax of the story? Explain your choice.
8. Explain how the title of each section is appropriate.

Critical

9. Explain the significance of the structure of *The Red Pony*.
10. Are Jody's actions believably motivated? Explain why or why not.
11. Compare and contrast Gitano and Grandfather.
12. Characterize John Steinbeck's style of writing. How does it contribute to the value of the novel?
13. What function does the character of Gitano serve in the novel?
14. Trace Jody's development through the four sections of the story.
15. Discuss Jody's relationship with his father and with Billy Buck.
16. Discuss Jody's relationship with his mother and with his grandfather.

Critical/Personal Response

17. If this story were told in the first person narrative by Jody, how would the story and its effect have changed?
18. Suppose Jody would tell about the events of the story at age 25. What do you think he would say?
19. *The Red Pony* is a short novel. Could anything have been gained by including more scenes from the time before or after the events of the story? If so, what could have been added and for what purpose. If not, explain why not.

Personal Response

20. Did you enjoy reading *The Red Pony*? Why or why not?
21. Jody had a special place he went when he wanted to be alone. Describe a place you like to go and explain why you like it there.
22. Define the word "old."
23. Grandfather thought that Americans have lost the pioneering spirit. What do you think?

VOCABULARY REVIEW ACTIVITIES

1. Divide your class into two teams and have an old-fashioned spelling or definition bee.

2. Give each of your students (or students in groups of two, three or four) a *The Red Pony* Vocabulary Word Search Puzzle. The person (group) to find all of the vocabulary words in the puzzle first wins.

3. Give students a *The Red Pony* Vocabulary Word Search Puzzle without the word list. The person or group to find the most vocabulary words in the puzzle wins.

4. Use a *The Red Pony* Vocabulary Crossword Puzzle. Put the puzzle onto a transparency on the overhead projector (so everyone can see it), and do the puzzle together as a class.

5. Give students a *The Red Pony* Vocabulary Matching Worksheet to do.

6. Divide your class into two teams. Use *The Red Pony* vocabulary words with their letters jumbled as a word list. Student 1 from Team A faces off against Student 1 from Team B. You write the first jumbled word on the board. The first student (1A or 1B) to unscramble the word wins the chance for his/her team to score points. If 1A wins the jumble, go to student 2A and give him/her a definition. He/she must give you the correct spelling of the vocabulary word which fits that definition. If he/she does, Team A scores a point, and you give student 3A a definition for which you expect a correctly spelled matching vocabulary word. Continue giving Team A definitions until some team member makes an incorrect response. An incorrect response sends the game back to the jumbled-word face off, this time with students 2A and 2B. Instead of repeating giving definitions to the first few students of each team, continue with the student after the one who gave the last incorrect response on the team. For example, if Team B wins the jumbled-word face-off, and student 5B gave the last incorrect answer for Team B, you would start this round of definition questions with student 6B, and so on. The team with the most points wins!

7. Have students write a story in which they correctly use as many vocabulary words as possible. Have students read their compositions orally! Post the most original compositions on your bulletin board!

LESSONS TEN AND ELEVEN

Objectives
1. To give students the opportunity to practice public speaking
2. To have students share their information so all students are exposed to a wide variety of thoughts and information
3. To conclude the unit projects

Activity
Have each group make its presentation to the class.

LESSONS TWELVE AND THIRTEEN

Objective
To trace the themes and ideas of the book through all four sections

Activity
Divide the class into groups of four people. Each group should be assigned one theme: Life versus death, youth versus age, Jody's "coming of age," Jody's relationship with Billy and Mr. Tiflin or Mrs. Tiflin's role in the novel. It doesn't matter if two or more groups have the same theme, as long as all the themes are covered by at least one group.

Students within the group will each take one chapter of *The Red Pony* and find all the references to their group's theme in that chapter. Students should jot down their findings. When the individuals are done with their research, group members should discuss their findings and (based on their research) try to draw some conclusions about the theme.

If you have two or more groups doing the same theme, give them a chance to combine their information and talk about their theme as a large group prior to the report segment. That way, you can have just one report about each theme. Use the group reports as springboards for discussions about the themes.

LESSON FOURTEEN

Objectives
1. To give students the opportunity to practice writing to persuade
2. To give the teacher the opportunity to evaluate students' writing skills

Activity
Distribute Writing Assignment #3. Discuss the directions in detail and give students ample time to complete the assignment.

NOTE: While students are working on Writing Assignment #3, call individual students to your desk or some other private area for a writing conference based on the first (and second) writing assignment(s). An evaluation form is included in this unit for your convenience.

WRITING ASSIGNMENT #3 - *The Red Pony*

PROMPT

Occasionally a good fairy drops something really wonderful in our laps, but most of the time if there is something we really want, we have to work for it -- figure out how we can get it and take the necessary steps to reach our goals. One good tool to have in your personal resources is the tool of being able to speak and/or write persuasively. This, too, like making promises, is learned at an early age; "Mommy, if I'm a really good boy could I please have a cookie?" (Said, of course, with big eyes, a smile, and a large halo over our little heads!) What mother could refuse?

Your assignment is to think of something you want and write a persuasive letter to the person who would be responsible for granting your wish.

PREWRITING

First, think of something you want. It could be a new bicycle, tickets to a concert, permission to go somewhere with your friend(s) -- anything that could be granted to you by someone.

Why do you want this thing? List several good reasons. What benefits does this thing have? List several. What possible objections could the person you are asking have--why would that person not want you to have it? What could you say or do to overcome the objections the person might have? Jot down those ideas, at least one solution for each objection.

DRAFTING

Use a letter format. If the person is someone you know well, use an informal letter. If the person is someone you do not know well or is in an official position of authority, use a formal business letter format.

Write an introductory paragraph in which you introduce what it is you want.

Write one paragraph for each of the reasons why you want it and what benefits it would have.

Write at least one paragraph in which you acknowledge the person's possible objections and give possible solutions to those objections. (For example, "I know you don't want me to be out late at night; I could be home by ten o'clock.") If there are many objections and solutions, adjust your paragraphing accordingly.

Write a concluding paragraph in which you restate what it is you want, and briefly recap the benefits, and your solutions to the objections.

PROOFREADING

When you finish the rough draft of your paper, ask a student who sits near you to read it. After reading your rough draft, he/she should tell you what he/she liked best about your work, which parts were difficult to understand, and ways in which your work could be improved. Reread your paper considering your critic's comments, and make the corrections you think are necessary. Do a final proofreading of your paper double-checking your grammar, spelling, organization, and the clarity of your ideas.

WRITING EVALUATION FORM - *The Red Pony*

Name _____ Date _____

    Grade _____

Grammar: excellent   good   fair   poor

Spelling: excellent   good   fair   poor

Punctuation: excellent   good   fair   poor

Legibility: excellent   good   fair   poor

Strengths:

Weaknesses:

Comments/Suggestions:

LESSON FIFTEEN

Objective
    To review the main ideas presented in *The Red Pony*

Activity #1
    Choose one of the review games/activities included in this unit and spend your class period as outlined there. Some materials for these activities are located in the Extra Activities section of this unit.

Activity #2
    Remind students that the Unit Test will be in the next class meeting. Stress the review of the Study Guides and their class notes as a last minute, brush-up review for homework.

REVIEW GAMES/ACTIVITIES - *The Red Pony*

1. Ask the class to make up a unit test for *The Red Pony*. The test should have 4 sections: matching, true/false, short answer, and essay. Students may use 1/2 period to make the test and then swap papers and use the other 1/2 class period to take a test a classmate has devised. (open book) You may want to use the unit test included in this unit or take questions from the students' unit tests to formulate your own test.

2. Take 1/2 period for students to make up true and false questions (including the answers). Collect the papers and divide the class into two teams. Draw a big tic-tac-toe board on the chalk board. Make one team X and one team O. Ask questions to each side, giving each student one turn. If the question is answered correctly, that student's team's letter (X or O) is placed in the box. If the answer is incorrect, no mark is placed in the box. The object is to get three marks in a row like tic-tac-toe. You may want to keep track of the number of games won for each team.

3. Take 1/2 period for students to make up questions (true/false and short answer). Collect the questions. Divide the class into two teams. You'll alternate asking questions to individual members of teams A & B (like in a spelling bee). The question keeps going from A to B until it is correctly answered, then a new question is asked. A correct answer does not allow the team to get another question. Correct answers are +2 points; incorrect answers are -1 point.

4. Have students pair up and quiz each other from their study guides and class notes.

5. Give students a *The Red Pony* crossword puzzle to complete.

6. Divide your class into two teams. Use *The Red Pony* crossword words with their letters jumbled as a word list. Student 1 from Team A faces off against Student 1 from Team B. You write the first jumbled word on the board. The first student (1A or 1B) to unscramble the word wins the chance for his/her team to score points. If 1A wins the jumble, go to student 2A and give him/her a clue. He/she must give you the correct word which matches that clue. If he/she does, Team A scores a point, and you give student 3A a clue for which you expect another correct response. Continue giving Team A clues until some team member makes an incorrect response. An incorrect response sends the game back to the jumbled-word face off, this time with students 2A and 2B. Instead of repeating giving clues to the first few students of each team, continue with the student after the one who gave the last incorrect response on the team. For example, if Team B wins the jumbled-word face-off, and student 5B gave the last incorrect answer for Team B, you would start this round of clue questions with student 6B, and so on. The team with the most points wins!

UNIT TESTS

SHORT ANSWER UNIT TEST 1 - *The Red Pony*

I. Matching

____ 1. Billy Buck   A. Author

____ 2. Carl   B. Black ___; the colt

____ 3. Demon   C. Mexican who came home to die

____ 4. Easter   D. Mare who died berthing

____ 5. Gabilan   E. Story teller who thought Americans had lost the pioneering spirit

____ 6. Gitano   F. Ranch hand; he became fallible

____ 7. Jody   G. Carl's old horse

____ 8. Nellie   H. The pony was a gift to him

____ 9. Steinbeck   I. The red pony

____ 10. Grandfather   J. Mr. Tiflin

II. Short Answer

1. What was the gift?

2. "Billy looked away . . . . He had no right to be fallible, and he knew it." Explain.

3. Why were the mountains "dear to him, and terrible."

Red Pony Short Answer Unit Test 1 Page 2

4. What was the promise?

5. What happened to Nellie?

6. Who was the leader of the people? Why was he called that?

7. What was Carl Tiflin's attitude towards Grandfather? Billy's? Jody's?

8. Why does Jody decide to kill the mice another day?

9. What ties together the four sections of this book?

Red Pony Short Answer Unit Test 1 Page 3

III. Composition: Answer each of the following in paragraph form:

1. List three main themes in *The Red Pony* and give a brief explanation of each.

2. Describe Billy's relationship with Jody.

3. Describe Carl Tiflin's relationship with Billy.

4. Discuss Mrs. Tiflin's role in the novel.

Red Pony Short Answer Unit Test 1 Page 4

IV. Vocabulary

Listen to the vocabulary words and write them down. Go back later and fill in the correct definition for each word.

1.

2.

3.

4.

5.

6.

7.

8.

9.

10.

KEY: SHORT ANSWER UNIT TEST #1 - *The Red Pony*

I. Matching

_F_ 1. Billy Buck   A. Author

_J_ 2. Carl   B. Black ___; the colt

_B_ 3. Demon   C. Mexican who came home to die

_G_ 4. Easter   D. Mare who died berthing

_I_ 5. Gabilan   E. Story teller who thought Americans had lost the pioneering spirit

_C_ 6. Gitano   F. Ranch hand; he became fallible

_H_ 7. Jody   G. Carl's old horse

_D_ 8. Nellie   H. The pony was a gift to him

_A_ 9. Steinbeck   I. The red pony

_E_ 10. Grandfather   J. Mr. Tiflin

II. Short Answer

1. What was the gift?
    The gift was Gabilan, the red pony.

2. "Billy looked away . . . . He had no right to be fallible, and he knew it." Explain.
    Billy made very few errors concerning the animals. Jody trusted him completely, admired and respected him. To Jody, Billy could do no wrong, and Billy knew Jody felt this way.

3. Why were the mountains "dear to him, and terrible."
    They were a mysterious place he thought he would like to see, and yet they also held the fear of the unknown.

4. What was the promise?
    Billy promised Jody he would see that he got a good colt.

5. What happened to Nellie?
   Billy Buck had to kill her to save the colt he had promised Jody.

6. Who was the leader of the people? Why was he called that?
   Jody's grandfather was the leader of the people. He had helped to bring a group of settlers west.

7. What was Carl Tiflin's attitude towards Grandfather? Billy's? Jody's?
   Mr. Tiflin is cold towards the grandfather. He doesn't want him there and doesn't even try to be polite. Billy doesn't particularly like the old man's company, but he at least tries to be polite. Jody likes the old man's stories and is really glad to have him there.

8. Why does Jody decide to kill the mice another day?
   Jody decides to kill the mice another day because he knows grandfather is feeling low. Killing the mice wouldn't be fun anymore.

9. What ties together the four sections of this book?
   All of the episodes in the book are tied together by Jody's coming of age. Each section shows how, through that particular experience, Jody grows into a young adult.

III. Composition: Answers will vary

IV. Vocabulary
   Choose ten of the vocabulary words to read orally for Part IV of the unit test:

SHORT ANSWER UNIT TEST 2 - *The Red Pony*

I. Matching

___ 1. Billy Buck   A. Mare who died berthing

___ 2. Carl   B. The red pony

___ 3. Demon   C. Carl's old horse

___ 4. Easter   D. Ranch hand; he became fallible

___ 5. Gabilan   E. Mr. Tiflin

___ 6. Gitano   F. Author

___ 7. Jody   G. Mexican who came home to die

___ 8. Nellie   H. The pony was a gift to him

___ 9. Steinbeck   I. Black ___; the colt

___ 10. Grandfather   J. Story teller who thought Americans had lost the pioneering spirit

II. Short Answer

1. What was the reaction of the six boys to Jody after he got his pony?

2. How did Jody change after he got the pony?

3. Describe Billy's relationship with Jody.

4. "Billy looked away. . . . He had no right to be fallible and he knew it." Explain.

Red Pony Short Answer Unit Test 2 Page 2

5. How did Mr. Tiflin react to Jody when he found him with the pony and buzzard? How did Billy react?

6. Why were the mountains "dear to him [Jody], and terrible"?

7. What was "the promise"?

8. What's Mr. Tiflin's attitude towards Grandfather?

9. What does Mrs. Tiflin realize about Jody when he asks for only one lemon?

10. List three main themes in *The Red Pony* and give a brief explanation of each.

Red Pony Short Answer Unit Test 2 Page 3

III. Composition

> Explain how the title of each section of the book is appropriate in terms of structure of the novel, the themes and in Jody's development.

IV. Vocabulary

> Listen to the vocabulary words and write them down. Go back later and fill in the correct definition for each word.

1.

2.

3.

4.

5.

6.

7.

8.

9.

10.

KEY: SHORT ANSWER UNIT TEST 2 *The Red Pony*

I. Matching (Use this matching key for the Advanced Short Answer Unit Test, too.)

__D__ 1. Billy Buck   A. Mare who died berthing

__E__ 2. Carl   B. The red pony

__I__ 3. Demon   C. Carl's old horse

__C__ 4. Easter   D. Ranch hand; he became fallible

__B__ 5. Gabilan   E. Mr. Tiflin

__G__ 6. Gitano   F. Author

__H__ 7. Jody   G. Mexican who came home to die

__A__ 8. Nellie   H. The pony was a gift to him

__F__ 9. Steinbeck   I. Black ___; the colt

__J__ 10. Grandfather   J. Story teller who thought Americans had lost the pioneering spirit

II. Short Answer

1. What was the reaction of the six boys to Jody after he got his pony?
    The boys had more admiration for Jody. He was better than they were because he had the pony.
2. How did Jody change after he got the pony?
    He rose promptly in the morning and did all of his chores without being told to do them. He acted more like an adult.
3. Describe Billy's relationship with Jody.
    Billy was a good friend and a father figure for Jody.
4. "Billy looked away. . . . He had no right to be fallible and he knew it." Explain.
    Billy made very few errors concerning the animals. Jody trusted him completely, admired and respected him. To Jody, Billy could do no wrong, and Billy knew Jody felt this way.

5. How did Mr. Tiflin react to Jody when he found him with the pony and buzzard? How did Billy react?

    Carl Tiflin was not particularly understanding. He only dealt with the obvious fact that the buzzard didn't kill the pony. He missed the point. Billy was concerned with Jody's feelings and had picked him up to take him home.

6. Why were the mountains "dear to him [Jody], and terrible"?

    They were a mysterious place he thought he would like to see, and yet they also held the fear of the unknown.

7. What was "the promise"?

    Billy promised Jody he would see that he got a good colt.

8. What's Mr. Tiflin's attitude towards Grandfather?

    Mr. Tiflin is cold towards the grandfather. He doesn't want him there and doesn't even try to be polite.

9. What does Mrs. Tiflin realize about Jody when he asks for only one lemon?

    She realizes that Jody has grown up a great deal. He thinks totally of grandfather's wants and not at all of his own.

10. List three main themes in *The Red Pony* and give a brief explanation of each.

    a. **life and death**: Steinbeck shows the life cycle in several ways. The pony, Gabilan, dies but becomes food (life) for the buzzards. The old Mexican man, Gitano, comes back to his homeland to die in the mountains (along with Easter, the old horse). Nellie dies giving birth to the new colt.

    b. **youth and age**: Again, there are several examples. Two prime ones are Gitano's knowledge vs. Jody's curiosity and wonder about the mountains and the fact that Grandfather recognizes his time is passing just as Jody is blossoming into early manhood.

    c. **coming of age**: The theme of Jody's coming of age is what holds the stories together. Each story shows how Jody grows as a result of his experiences. The final comment on his growth was his willingness to get his grandfather a drink of lemonade even though he personally did not want any.

III. Composition: Answers will vary.

IV. Vocabulary: Choose ten of the vocabulary words to dictate to your students in this section of the test.

ADVANCED SHORT ANSWER UNIT TEST - *The Red Pony*

I. Matching

___ 1. Billy Buck   A. Mare who died berthing

___ 2. Carl   B. The red pony

___ 3. Demon   C. Carl's old horse

___ 4. Easter   D. Ranch hand; he became fallible

___ 5. Gabilan   E. Mr. Tiflin

___ 6. Gitano   F. Author

___ 7. Jody   G. Mexican who came home to die

___ 8. Nellie   H. The pony was a gift to him

___ 9. Steinbeck   I. Black ___; the colt

___ 10. Grandfather   J. Story teller who thought Americans had lost the pioneering spirit

II. Short Answer

1. What are three main themes in *The Red Pony*. Give a short description of each.

Red Pony Advanced Short Answer Unit Test Page 2

2. Explain how the titles of each section of the book are appropriate in terms of the action within the section, in relation to Jody's growth, and in relation to the theme developments.

3. What are the main conflicts in *The Red Pony*? Are they all resolved? If so, how? If not, why not?

4. Describe Jody's relationships with the following characters:
   a. Carl

   b. Billy

   c. Grandfather

Red Pony Advanced Short Answer Unit Test Page 3

5. List three specific events (in order) that showed Jody's growth.

6. Was Carl Tiflin a good father? Defend your answer.

III. Composition

What point(s) do you think John Steinbeck was making when he wrote *The Red Pony*? What are we supposed to gain from reading it?

Red Pony Advanced Short Answer Unit Test Page 4

IV. Vocabulary

    Listen to the vocabulary words and write them down. Go back later and write a composition in which you use all of the words. The composition must relate in some way to *The Red Pony*.

MULTIPLE CHOICE UNIT TEST 1 - *The Red Pony*

I. Matching

____ 1. Billy Buck   A. Author

____ 2. Carl   B. Black ___; the colt

____ 3. Demon   C. Mexican who came home to die

____ 4. Easter   D. Mare who died berthing

____ 5. Gabilan   E. Story teller who thought Americans had lost the pioneering spirit

____ 6. Gitano   F. Ranch hand; he became fallible

____ 7. Jody   G. Carl's old horse

____ 8. Nellie   H. The pony was a gift to him

____ 9. Steinbeck   I. The red pony

____ 10. Grandfather   J. Mr. Tiflin

II. Multiple Choice

1. What was the reaction of the six boys to Jody after Jody got the pony?
    a. They were jealous, so they ignored him.
    b. They were not particularly interested, because they all had their own ponies.
    c. They had more admiration, because having a pony made him better than they were.
    d. They all wanted to be his friend so that he would give them rides.

2. How did Jody change after he got the pony?
    a. He rose promptly in the morning and did all of his chores without being told to.
    b. He became obsessed with the pony and ignored his chores and schoolwork.
    c. He became moody and sullen.
    d. He let his school work go, and his grades dropped.

Red Pony Multiple Choice Unit Test 1 Page 2

3. Describe Billy's relationship with Jody.
    a. Billy was distant and cool.
    b. Billy competed with Jody for Carl's attention.
    c. Billy was a good friend and a father figure.
    d. Billy was deferential to Jody because he was the boss's son.

4. Who visited the Tiflin farm and why did he come?
    a. The school principal came because Jody was misbehaving.
    b. An old man, Gitano, came back to his home-place to die.
    c. Billy's cousin from the East came to visit for a few months.
    d. Billy's brother came to visit on his way to Los Angeles.

5. "Carl was afraid he might relent and let the old man stay, and so he continued to remind himself that this couldn't be." What do we learn about Mr. Tiflin's character through this passage? What kind of a man is he?
    a. He is more compassionate than he would let himself show.
    b. He is indecisive and weak.
    c. He is paranoid.
    d. He is self-centered.

6. What deal does Jody make with his father in order to have the mare bred?
    a. He must get straight As on his report card.
    b. He has to go to church without complaining for six months.
    c. He has to do extra chores.
    d. He has to sell his dog.

7. What kinds of daydreams did Jody have about the colt?
    a. He kept dreaming that the colt would die.
    b. He fantasized about being a larger-than-life hero.
    c. He dreamed that the colt was so wild even he couldn't ride it, and he never enjoyed having it.
    d. He thought about traveling the world, and charging people money to watch his "wonder horse" do tricks. In his daydreams he got very rich.

Red Pony Multiple Choice Unit Test 1 Page 3

8. What was "the promise?"
    a. Billy promised Jody he would get a good colt.
    b. Jody promised his parents he would always do his schoolwork and chores first, before playing with the colt.
    c. Mr. Tiflin promised Jody a new saddle when the colt was three years old.
    d. Mrs. Tiflin promised to make Jody a special riding outfit after the colt was born.

9. What do we learn about Jody after the birth of the colt?
    a. He is still a self-centered, spoiled little boy who always puts himself first.
    b. He is starting to think about other people.
    c. He isn't very smart.
    d. He is odd.

10. Who was the Leader of the People?
    a. It was the governor of California.
    b. It was the last remaining chief of the Salinas Indian tribe.
    c. It was Mrs. Tiflin's father.
    d. It was Jody's new name for Billy.

11. What is Mr. Tiflin's attitude towards Grandfather?
    a. He welcomed him and enjoyed his company.
    b. He refused to have him in the house.
    c. He was afraid of the older man, and tolerated him.
    d. He was cold and impolite.

12. What was Jody's attitude towards Grandfather?
    a. He is glad to have him.
    b. He resents sharing the attention of his parents.
    c. He thinks the old man is stupid and senile.
    d. He is angry because he has to give up his bed.

13. What does Mrs. Tiflin realize about Jody when he asks for only one lemon?
    a. He is very depressed.
    b. His tastes are changing.
    c. He is acting more and more like his father.
    d. He is thinking of someone else instead of himself.

Red Pony Multiple Choice Unit Test 1 Page 4

III. Composition

    Explain why Jody is the central character of the story.

Red Pony Multiple Choice Unit Test 1 Page 5

IV. Vocabulary - Match the correct definitions to the words.

_____ 1. RAMBUNCTIOUSNESS   A. Distant; indifferent; apart

_____ 2. POTENTIAL   B. Haughty; contemptuous; overbearing

_____ 3. ALOOF   C. An image that appears only in the mind; ghost

_____ 4. STAUNCHNESS   D. Prevented action or progress; impeded

_____ 5. LISTLESSLY   E. Threateningly

_____ 6. PARALLEL   F. Indifferently; unenthusiastically

_____ 7. CONTEMPLATIVE   G. In a fatherly manner

_____ 8. VICINITY   H. Take back; withdraw

_____ 9. HAMPERED   I. Characteristic of not capable of being upset

_____ 10. RETRACT   J. Gotten rid of; left out of consideration

_____ 11. LANGUOROUS   K. Steadfastness; resoluteness

_____ 12. PHANTOM   L. Explained; interpreted

_____ 13. DISCONSOLATELY   M. Equal distance apart at all points; a comparison indicating similarities

_____ 14. ARROGANT   N. Sorrowfully; dejectedly

_____ 15. PATERNALLY   O. Still; sluggish; listless

_____ 16. COMPLACENT   P. Locality; proximity; neighborhood

_____ 17. CONSTRUED   Q. Boisterousness; rowdiness

_____ 18. IMPERTURBABILITY   R. Thoughtful; meditative

_____ 19. OMINOUSLY   S. Self-satisfied; contented

_____ 20. ELIMINATED   T. Latent; possible but not yet so

MULTIPLE CHOICE UNIT TEST 2 - *The Red Pony*

I. Matching

____ 1. Billy Buck   A. Mare who died berthing

____ 2. Carl   B. The red pony

____ 3. Demon   C. Carl's old horse

____ 4. Easter   D. Ranch hand; he became fallible

____ 5. Gabilan   E. Mr. Tiflin

____ 6. Gitano   F. Author

____ 7. Jody   G. Mexican who came home to die

____ 8. Nellie   H. The pony was a gift to him

____ 9. Steinbeck   I. Black ___; the colt

____ 10. Grandfather   J. Story teller who thought Americans had lost the pioneering spirit

II. Multiple Choice

1. What was the reaction of the six boys to Jody after Jody got the pony?
    a. They had more admiration, because having a pony made him better than they were.
    b. They were jealous, so they ignored him.
    c. They were not particularly interested, because they all had their own ponies.
    d. They all wanted to be his friend so that he would give them rides.

2. How did Jody change after he got the pony?
    a. He became moody and sullen.
    b. He let his school work go, and his grades dropped.
    c. He became obsessed with the pony and ignored his chores and schoolwork.
    d. He rose promptly in the morning and did all of his chores without being told to.

Red Pony Multiple Choice Unit Test 2 Page 2

3. Describe Billy's relationship with Jody.
    a. Billy competed with Jody for Carl's attention.
    b. Billy was a good friend and a father figure.
    c. Billy was deferential to Jody because he was the boss's son.
    d. Billy was distant and cool.

4. Who visited the Tiflin farm and why did he come?
    a. Billy's brother came to visit on his way to Los Angeles.
    b. The school principal came because Jody was misbehaving.
    c. An old man, Gitano, came back to his home-place to die.
    d. Billy's cousin from the East came to visit for a few months.

5. "Carl was afraid he might relent and let the old man stay, and so he continued to remind himself that this couldn't be." What do we learn about Mr. Tiflin's character through this passage? What kind of a man is he?
    a. He is paranoid.
    b. He is indecisive and weak.
    c. He is self-centered.
    d. He is more compassionate than he would let himself show.

6. What deal does Jody make with his father in order to have the mare bred?
    a. He has to sell his dog.
    b. He has to go to church without complaining for six months.
    c. He must get straight As on his report card.
    d. He has to do extra chores.

7. What kinds of daydreams did Jody have about the colt?
    a. He thought about traveling the world, and charging people money to watch his "wonder horse" do tricks. In his daydreams he got very rich.
    b. He kept dreaming that the colt would die.
    c. He fantasized about being a larger-than-life hero.
    d. He dreamed that the colt was so wild even he couldn't ride it, and he never enjoyed having it.

Red Pony Multiple Choice Unit Test 2 Page 3

8. What was "the promise?"
    a. Jody promised his parents he would always do his schoolwork and chores first, before playing with the colt.
    b. Mr. Tiflin promised Jody a new saddle when the colt was three years old.
    c. Billy promised Jody he would get a good colt.
    d. Mrs. Tiflin promised to make Jody a special riding outfit after the colt was born.

9. What do we learn about Jody after the birth of the colt?
    a. He is starting to think about other people.
    b. He is still a self-centered, spoiled little boy who always puts himself first.
    c. He is odd.
    d. He isn't very smart.

10. Who was the Leader of the People?
    a. It was Mrs. Tiflin's father.
    b. It was Jody's new name for Billy.
    c. It was the last remaining chief of the Salinas Indian tribe.
    d. It was the governor of California.

11. What is Mr. Tiflin's attitude towards Grandfather?
    a. He refused to have him in the house.
    b. He was cold and impolite.
    c. He welcomed him and enjoyed his company.
    d. He was afraid of the older man, and tolerated him.

12. What was Jody's attitude towards Grandfather?
    a. He resents sharing the attention of his parents.
    b. He thinks the old man is stupid and senile.
    c. He is glad to have him.
    d. He is angry because he has to give up his bed.

13. What does Mrs. Tiflin realize about Jody when he asks for only one lemon?
    a. He is acting more and more like his father.
    b. His tastes are changing.
    c. He is thinking of someone else instead of himself.
    d. He is very depressed.

Red Pony Multiple Choice Unit Test 2 Page 4

III. Composition

Explain why Jody is the central character of the story.

Red Pony Multiple Choice Unit Test 2 Page 5

IV. Vocabulary - Match the correct definitions to the words.

____ 1. CONTEMPLATIVE   A. Assembled; came together

____ 2. CONTEMPTUOUSLY   B. With a lack of concern; showing indifference

____ 3. MARTIALLY   C. Suddenly

____ 4. PATERNALLY   D. Made a low, dull, monotonous sound

____ 5. DRONED   E. Steadfastness; resoluteness

____ 6. RETRACT   F. Still; sluggish; listless

____ 7. ABRUPTLY   G. Continually

____ 8. PERPETUALLY   H. Belittlingly; reducing in esteem

____ 9. CONSTRUED   I. Take back; withdraw

____ 10. PARALLEL   J. With complexly arranged elements

____ 11. STAUNCHNESS   K. Thoughtful; meditative

____ 12. CONVENED   L. Energetically; vigorously; actively

____ 13. STRENUOUSLY   M. In a fatherly manner

____ 14. INCENSED   N. In a military or warlike manner

____ 15. INTRICATELY   O. Haughty; contemptuous; overbearing

____ 16. LANGUOROUS   P. Self-satisfied; contented

____ 17. DISPARAGINGLY   Q. Disdainfully; scornfully

____ 18. NONCHALANCE   R. Enraged; angered

____ 19. ARROGANT   S. Equal distance apart at all points; a comparison indicating similarities

____ 20. COMPLACENT   T. Explained; interpreted

ANSWER SHEET
Multiple Choice Unit Tests
The Red Pony

I. Matching
1. ___
2. ___
3. ___
4. ___
5. ___
6. ___
7. ___
8. ___
9. ___
10. ___

II. Multiple Choice
1. ___
2. ___
3. ___
4. ___
5. ___
6. ___
7. ___
8. ___
9. ___
10. ___
11. ___
12. ___
13. ___

IV. Vocabulary
1. ___
2. ___
3. ___
4. ___
5. ___
6. ___
7. ___
8. ___
9. ___
10. ___
11. ___
12. ___
13. ___
14. ___
15. ___
16. ___
17. ___
18. ___
19. ___
20. ___

ANSWER KEY - *The Red Pony*
Multiple Choice Unit Tests

Answers to Unit Test 1 are in the left column. Answers to Unit Test 2 are in the right column.

I. Matching	II. Multiple Choice	IV. Vocabulary
1. F D	1. C A	1. Q K
2. J E	2. A D	2. T Q
3. B I	3. C B	3. A N
4. G C	4. B C	4. K M
5. I B	5. A D	5. F D
6. C G	6. C D	6. M I
7. H H	7. B C	7. R C
8. D A	8. A C	8. P G
9. A F	9. B A	9. D T
10. E J	10. C A	10. H S
	11. D B	11. O E
	12. A C	12. C A
	13. D C	13. N L
		14. B R
		15. G J
		16. S F
		17. L H
		18. I B
		19. E O
		20. J P

UNIT RESOURCE MATERIALS

BULLETIN BOARD IDEAS - *The Red Pony*

1. Save one corner of the board for the best of student's *The Red Pony* writing assignments.

2. Take one of the word search puzzles from the extra activities section and with a marker copy it over in a large size on the bulletin board. Write the clue words to find to one side. Invite students prior to and after class to find the words and circle them on the bulletin board.

3. Write several of the most significant quotations from the book onto the board on brightly colored paper.

4. Make a bulletin board listing the vocabulary words for this unit. As you complete sections of the novel and discuss the vocabulary for each section, write the definitions on the bulletin board. (If your board is one students face frequently, it will help them learn the words.)

5. Bring in or have students bring in pictures of farm life from magazines. Make a collage if you have enough different pictures (or post individual pictures on colorful paper if you only have a few pictures). This could also be a fun introductory activity if students participate. You could have the border and title done for the bulletin board and invite students to staple up their own pictures wherever they want them. It will take a few minutes of class time, but the students will enjoy it and you can get your bulletin board done in a hurry.

6. Use the same idea as in #5, but instead of farm life pictures, use pictures of kids from ten to teens, roughly Jody's age in the novel. Title the board something like: *The Red Pony*: Coming of Age.

7. Use pictures contrasting youth and age and/or life and death. Position the pictures so the contrast is clearly shown, perhaps coordinating the color of the background paper or using yarn to connect the contrasting pictures. Title the board *The Red Pony*: The Life Cycle.

8. Divide your board into four sections: Gifts, Mountains, Promises, and Leaders of the People. Post pictures appropriate for each of the sections.

EXTRA ACTIVITIES - *The Red Pony*

One of the difficulties in teaching a novel is that all students don't read at the same speed. One student who likes to read may take the book home and finish it in a day or two. Sometimes a few students finish the in-class assignments early. The problem, then, is finding suitable extra activities for students.

The best thing I've found is to keep a little library in the classroom. For this unit on *The Red Pony*, you might check out from the school library other related books and articles about farm life, training (also raising or riding) horses, the elderly in our society, growing up, careers in agriculture or veterinary science, or articles of criticism about *The Red Pony*. A biography of John Steinbeck would be interesting for some students to read. Other works by John Steinbeck would also make good additions to your in-class library.

Other things you may keep on hand are puzzles. We have made some relating directly to *The Red Pony* for you. Feel free to duplicate them.

Some students may like to draw. You might devise a contest or allow some extra-credit grade for students who draw characters or scenes from *The Red Pony*. Note, too, that if the students do not want to keep their drawings you may pick up some extra bulletin board materials this way. If you have a contest and you supply the prize, you could, possibly, make the drawing itself a non-returnable entry fee.

The pages which follow contain games, puzzles and worksheets. The keys, when appropriate, immediately follow the puzzle or worksheet. There are two main groups of activities: one group for the unit; that is, generally relating to *The Red Pony* text, and another group of activities related strictly to *The Red Pony* vocabulary.

Directions for these games, puzzles and worksheets are self-explanatory. The object here is to provide you with extra materials you may use in any way you choose.

MORE ACTIVITIES - *The Red Pony*

1. Pick a chapter or scene and have the students act it out on a stage. (Perhaps you could assign various scenes to different groups of students so more than one scene could be acted and more students could participate.)

2. Have a guest speaker come in to discuss modern ranching methods and problems.

3. Use some of the related topics noted earlier in the unit as topics for guest speakers or research papers.

4. Have students design a book cover (front and back and inside flaps) for *The Red Pony*.

5. Have students design a bulletin board (ready to be put up; not just sketched) for *The Red Pony*.

6. If you live in (or close to) a rural area where there are many farms or ranches, have a "show and tell" related to farm life so students can practice speaking in front of a group.

7. Hold a discussion about the differences between "real" ranching and the kind of ranching depicted in western movies and television shows.

8. Have students pretend they are Jody, and have them write a letter to Grandfather about his visit.

9. Have students write (and title) the next section that might follow Leader of the People.

WORD SEARCH - *The Red Pony*

All words in this list are associated with *The Red Pony* with an emphasis on the vocabulary words chosen for study in the text. The words are placed backwards, forward, diagonally, up and down. The included words are listed below.

```
Z D L N Z G F B E L V N P P K Z T Q Q W Y T X W
J W L D J P V X L V D B X Q H F Q L M N K T P C
X C F H H B W T D Y I R U Q S W W S M K Y N T S
M B N C C L G S D H R S E Z G N D Y W P C M Q Y
G S N K W F A R M E N E L D Z M E F O H Z K T D
W R K B M L V J E I M D S U A A Y L V N O R S F
G H A C I J T Y R T C O R I P E R Y B B A R V Y
F F T N O I L L A T S E N O M E L D G I F T S Z
B F A D C R T W R E D A N Y I L R N N D L N I E
X S Y Q A H E A R I L Y E D I C I I T O I L H G
X Y N C C S P O R I K K J B N R N N C A K B A X
F D S E I Y H P B C D K Y C E G I P T C N Q M F
Q H P M L C M A P Q M H D T V O M N E K T H G R
W F O P H L G W C L M M S H P G U B H H G P M L
H R N B N N I G Q B Q E L R Q O N Z X J D L T Z
P X M G T J V E Y Y W Z E J M I D Z Y J V Q V V
J Q R W W B Y T S W C T X C E L Y R J Q C C B K
L L P P Q G Z D Q D N W Z T J Y R Q K H D C R F
B N S Y Y L Q D M E N H S B J N Y T M F F M K D
B J T W F Q D B C Y T Q X S K T F K S P W F M M
```

BILLY	FALLIBLE	MISERY	ROCKS
BUZZARD	GABILAN	MOUNTAINS	SALINAS
CARL	GIFT	NELLIE	STALLION
CENTERPOINT	GITANO	PONY	STEINBECK
CHORES	HORSE	PRIDE	TRAINING
COLT	JODY	PROMISE	TRAP
DEMON	LEADER	RANCH	WESTERING
DIE	LEMON	RED	
EASTER	MICE	REPULSIVE	

KEY WORD SEARCH - *The Red Pony*

All words in this list are associated with *The Red Pony* with an emphasis on the vocabulary words chosen for study in the text. The words are placed backwards, forward, diagonally, up and down. The included words are listed below.

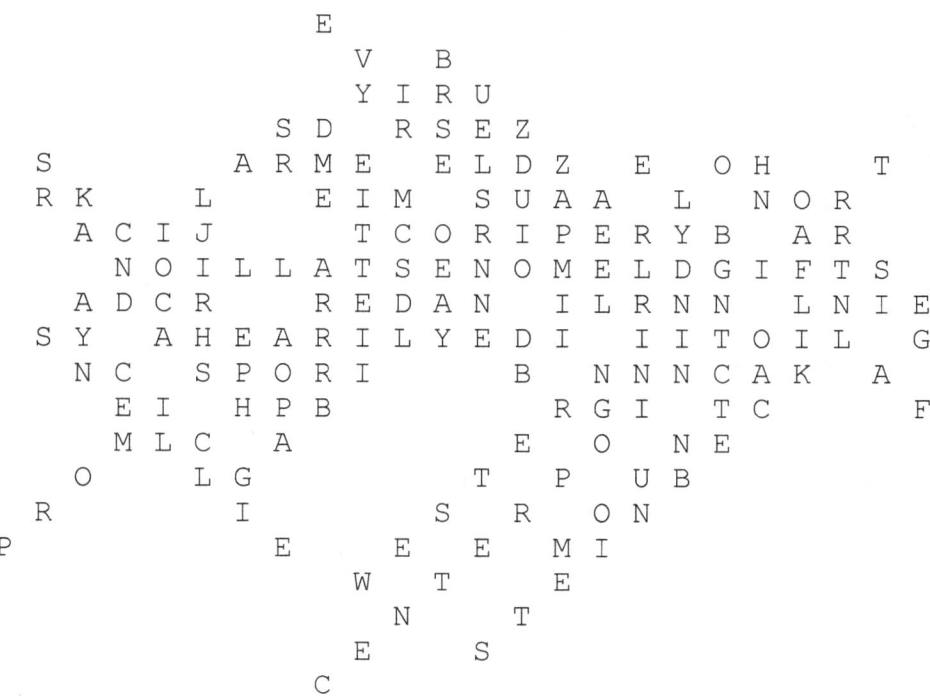

BILLY	FALLIBLE	MISERY	ROCKS
BUZZARD	GABILAN	MOUNTAINS	SALINAS
CARL	GIFT	NELLIE	STALLION
CENTERPOINT	GITANO	PONY	STEINBECK
CHORES	HORSE	PRIDE	TRAINING
COLT	JODY	PROMISE	TRAP
DEMON	LEADER	RANCH	WESTERING
DIE	LEMON	RED	
EASTER	MICE	REPULSIVE	

CROSSWORD - *The Red Pony*

CROSSWORD CLUES - *The Red Pony*

ACROSS

1. Mare who died berthing
3. Billy looked away....He had no right to be ____
5. Section I: The ____
7. Jody kills ____ in the haystack
9. Jobs Jody had to do on the ranch
13. Jody snapped a dog's nose in one
14. Animal house
16. Section IV: The ____ of the People
17. Mrs. Tiflin felt 'a curious ____ rise up in her'
18. Black ____; the colt
23. The brush line where there was a patch of perpetually green grass was Jody's ____
25. Old things ought to be put out of their ____
28. Carl had to --- to breed the mare; exchange money
29. ____ Buck; ranch hand
32. Mr. Tiflin sold cows & bought a pony there
33. Section II: The Great ____
34. Short novel
35. Coordinating conjunction
36. That's all; there is no more; the ---

DOWN

1. Negative reply
2. Jody asked for only one
4. Carl's old horse
5. Mexican man who came home to die
6. The red pony resented ____
8. Baby horse
10. Easter, for example
11. Color of the Pony
12. Place where Billy Buck works
15. Water from the sky
17. Section III: The ____
18. Gitano came home to do this
19. Another word for breed
20. The Red ____
21. Jody, for example; opposite of girl
22. He got a pony
23. Jody's father
24. The black cypress tree where pigs were slaughtered was ____ to Jody
26. Male horse
27. Jody threw them at birds
29. Jody beat it to death
30. Jody --- the pony; has strong feelings for
31. The red pony
32. In the near future

CROSSWORD ANSWER KEY - *The Red Pony*

MATCHING QUIZ/WORKSHEET 1 - *The Red Pony*

____ 1. MISERY   A. It has died out of the people

____ 2. HORSE   B. Old things ought to be put out of their ____

____ 3. MICE   C. Jody threw them at birds

____ 4. CENTERPOINT   D. The brush line where there was a patch of perpetually green grass was Jody's ____

____ 5. GITANO   E. He got a pony

____ 6. TRAP   F. Carl's old horse

____ 7. EASTER   G. Easter, for example

____ 8. RANCH   H. Jody kills ____ in the haystack

____ 9. RED   I. Place where Billy Buck works

____ 10. LEMON   J. Color of the Pony

____ 11. CARL   K. Jody beat it to death

____ 12. DIE   L. Mare who died berthing

____ 13. PONY   M. Black ____; the colt

____ 14. NELLIE   N. Billy looked away....He had no right to be ____

____ 15. WESTERING   O. Jody asked for only one

____ 16. ROCKS   P. Mexican man who came home to die

____ 17. FALLIBLE   Q. Jody snapped a dog's nose in one

____ 18. DEMON   R. Jody's father

____ 19. BUZZARD   S. The Red ____

____ 20. JODY   T. Gitano came home to do this

KEY: MATCHING QUIZ/WORKSHEET 1 - *The Red Pony*

__B_	1. MISERY	A. It has died out of the people
__G_	2. HORSE	B. Old things ought to be put out of their _____
__H_	3. MICE	C. Jody threw them at birds
__D_	4. CENTERPOINT	D. The brush line where there was a patch of perpetually green grass was Jody's _____
__P_	5. GITANO	E. He got a pony
__Q_	6. TRAP	F. Carl's old horse
__F_	7. EASTER	G. Easter, for example
__I_	8. RANCH	H. Jody kills ____ in the haystack
__J_	9. RED	I. Place where Billy Buck works
__O_	10. LEMON	J. Color of the Pony
__R_	11. CARL	K. Jody beat it to death
__T_	12. DIE	L. Mare who died berthing
__S_	13. PONY	M. Black ___; the colt
__L_	14. NELLIE	N. Billy looked away....He had no right to be ____
__A_	15. WESTERING	O. Jody asked for only one
__C_	16. ROCKS	P. Mexican man who came home to die
__N_	17. FALLIBLE	Q. Jody snapped a dog's nose in one
__M_	18. DEMON	R. Jody's father
__K_	19. BUZZARD	S. The Red ___
__E_	20. JODY	T. Gitano came home to do this

MATCHING QUIZ/WORKSHEET 2 - *The Red Pony*

____ 1. STEINBECK   A. Old things ought to be put out of their ____

____ 2. MISERY   B. Section I: The ____

____ 3. EASTER   C. Jody beat it to death

____ 4. MICE   D. The red pony resented ____

____ 5. BUZZARD   E. Carl's old horse

____ 6. CARL   F. Author

____ 7. COLT   G. Gitano came home to do this

____ 8. PROMISE   H. Section III: The ____

____ 9. PONY   I. Mr. Tiflin sold cows & bought a pony there

____ 10. REPULSIVE   J. The Red ____

____ 11. GIFT   K. Jody snapped a dog's nose in one

____ 12. RED   L. Mare who died berthing

____ 13. TRAINING   M. Section IV: The ____ of the People

____ 14. GABILAN   N. Jobs Jody had to do on the ranch

____ 15. SALINAS   O. Jody's father

____ 16. TRAP   P. The red pony

____ 17. LEADER   Q. Baby horse

____ 18. NELLIE   R. Color of the Pony

____ 19. CHORES   S. Jody kills ____ in the haystack

____ 20. DIE   T. The black cypress tree where pigs were slaughtered was ____ to Jody

KEY: MATCHING QUIZ/WORKSHEET 2 - *The Red Pony*

_F__	1. STEINBECK	A. Old things ought to be put out of their ____
_A__	2. MISERY	B. Section I: The ____
_E__	3. EASTER	C. Jody beat it to death
_S__	4. MICE	D. The red pony resented ____
_C__	5. BUZZARD	E. Carl's old horse
_O__	6. CARL	F. Author
_Q__	7. COLT	G. Gitano came home to do this
_H__	8. PROMISE	H. Section III: The ___
_J__	9. PONY	I. Mr. Tiflin sold cows & bought a pony there
_T__	10. REPULSIVE	J. The Red ___
_B__	11. GIFT	K. Jody snapped a dog's nose in one
_R__	12. RED	L. Mare who died berthing
_D__	13. TRAINING	M. Section IV: The ___ of the People
_P__	14. GABILAN	N. Jobs Jody had to do on the ranch
_I__	15. SALINAS	O. Jody's father
_K__	16. TRAP	P. The red pony
_M__	17. LEADER	Q. Baby horse
_L__	18. NELLIE	R. Color of the Pony
_N__	19. CHORES	S. Jody kills ____ in the haystack
_G__	20. DIE	T. The black cypress tree where pigs were slaughtered was ___ to Jody

JUGGLE LETTER REVIEW GAME CLUE SHEET - *The Red Pony*

SCRAMBLED	WORD	CLUE
LIYBL	BILLY	___ Buck; ranch hand
ZABZUDR	BUZZARD	Jody beat it to death
RALC	CARL	Jody's father
REPOTINNECT	CENTERPOINT	The brush line where there was a patch of perpetually green grass was Jody's ___
SHECOR	CHORES	Jobs Jody had to do on the ranch
TLOC	COLT	Baby horse
MODEN	DEMON	Black ___; the colt
IDE	DIE	Gitano came home to do this
TRASEE	EASTER	Carl's old horse
LEBLAFIL	FALLIBLE	Billy looked away....He had no right to be ___
BLAGINA	GABILAN	The red pony
FIGT	GIFT	Section I: The ___
INOGAT	GITANO	Mexican man who came home to die
ROSHE	HORSE	Easter, for example
YODJ	JODY	He got a pony
REDEAL	LEADER	Section IV: The ___ of the People
MOLEN	LEMON	Jody asked for only one
CIME	MICE	Jody kills ___ in the haystack
RIMYES	MISERY	Old things ought to be put out of their ___
TUMONASIN	MOUNTAINS	Section II: The Great ___
LEINEL	NELLIE	Mare who died berthing
NOPY	PONY	The Red ___
DRIPE	PRIDE	Mrs. Tiflin felt 'a curious ___ rise up in her'
SRIMOPE	PROMISE	Section III: The ___
HARNC	RANCH	Place where Billy Buck works
DER	RED	Color of the Pony
LIPERVUSE	REPULSIVE	The black cypress tree where pigs were slaughtered was ___ to Jody
SKORC	ROCKS	Jody threw them at birds
LASSAIN	SALINAS	Mr. Tiflin sold cows & bought a pony there
SLOTLINA	STALLION	Male horse
BETSICKEN	STEINBECK	Author
GANITIRN	TRAINING	The red pony resented ___
PRAT	TRAP	Jody snapped a dog's nose in one
REQETIGNNS	WESTERING	It has died out of the people

VOCABULARY RESOURCE MATERIALS

VOCABULARY WORD SEARCH - *The Red Pony*

All words in this list are associated with *The Red Pony* with an emphasis on the vocabulary words chosen for study in the text. The words are placed backwards, forward, diagonally, up and down. The included words are listed below.

```
I N T R I C A T E L Y L L A U T E P R E P T D Y
D T S N V P T H A L Y G H Y Y O Z C J L N E X R
C Q Y L A D D B S L G R Q L Y H M X S E T G L E
V Z R L Q G R U C W L F S L K L D I C A R M V B
S S E N S U O I T C N U B M A R A A N D C I G S
B W W Z P U W R T F O D P L O X L I E O T N H C
M Q H T N N O F R U K V W N T P M N T A U Z H S
H D L E L L M E T A S S E S M I E L L N N S P Y
C Y R S T F D P T M E D R O L V H P C Z E W L Y
Y T C S S T M R C I V G C E N I M A D N X T L Y
S C K M H E E O X C P Y I O Y E N R M W Y S O S
S X G W T B N D D A G F C T T P M C K P S R U P
L B M N S S Q H T K M S I N S A H T E E E O F H
S E O M T C W E C Y F N O X R E L A L N R R N R
N C L R Z M R N C N I C S T F J R T N O S P E M
R V U L K N K Z T C U B I L Z C S P U T L E N D
R E T R A C T D I S P A R A G I N G L Y O X D Q
D C P L M R R V G B L V T D L Z N T T S V M F R
T M L J P C A M Q L M F V S C A Y V N P C C L R
S Y A L O O F P Y V E C N A L A H C N O N J M C
```

ABRUPTLY	DISPARAGINGLY	MARTIALLY	POTENTIAL
ALOOF	DRONED	NONCHALANCE	PRESTIGE
ARROGANT	ELIMINATED	OMINOUSLY	RETRACT
COMPLACENT	HAMPERED	PARALLEL	STAUNCHNESS
CONSTRUED	INCENSED	PATERNALLY	STRENUOUSLY
CONTEMPLATIVE	INTRICATELY	PERPETUALLY	VICINITY
CONTEMPTUOUSLY	LANGUOROUS	PHANTOM	WHETTED
CONVENED	LISTLESSLY	PITEOUSLY	
RAMBUNCTIOUSNESS			

KEY: VOCABULARY WORD SEARCH - *The Red Pony*

All words in this list are associated with *The Red Pony* with an emphasis on the vocabulary words chosen for study in the text. The words are placed backwards, forward, diagonally, up and down. The included words are listed below.

```
        I N T R I C A T E L Y L L A U T E P R E P T D
            N           A L         Y O           N E
          Y   A       B S           L     M   E T       E
          L   G R U           S       L D I C A       V
    S S E N S U O I T C N U B M A R A A N D     I
      W     P   U   R     O         O   L I E O T
        H T N   O   R U       N     P M N T A U
        L E       E T A       E   M I E   L N       S
        Y R S     P T   E D   O L V H P       E     L Y
          T     S T M   C I   G C E N I M A       T L Y
    S           E E O       P   I O Y E N   M     S O S
                T   N D   A       C T T P M C   P S   U P
    L       N     S   H T         I N S A H     E E O
        E O     T       E C     N O     R E     A L N R R
        C L R     R       N I C     T       R T N O S       E
        U L   N         C U     I           S P U T     E     D
    R E T R A C T D I S P A R A G I N G L Y O     D
    D       L   R   V       L       T     L   N             M
            L       A     L         S   A
          Y A L O O F P Y     E C N A L A H C N O N
```

ABRUPTLY	DISPARAGINGLY	MARTIALLY	POTENTIAL
ALOOF	DRONED	NONCHALANCE	PRESTIGE
ARROGANT	ELIMINATED	OMINOUSLY	RETRACT
COMPLACENT	HAMPERED	PARALLEL	STAUNCHNESS
CONSTRUED	INCENSED	PATERNALLY	STRENUOUSLY
CONTEMPLATIVE	INTRICATELY	PERPETUALLY	VICINITY
CONTEMPTUOUSLY	LANGUOROUS	PHANTOM	WHETTED
CONVENED	LISTLESSLY	PITEOUSLY	
RAMBUNCTIOUSNESS			

VOCABULARY CROSSWORD - *The Red Pony*

VOCABULARY CROSSWORD CLUES - *The Red Pony*

ACROSS

1. Enraged; angered
7. Suddenly
9. Interior divisions of a house
10. Latent; possible but not yet so
14. Gitano came home to do this
15. Friends; pals; a pair
16. Negative reply
17. Stetson is a kind of cowboy ---
18. Made the acquaintance of
19. Still; sluggish; listless
20. Mare who died berthing
21. Zero; zilch
22. Neither's partner
23. Ingest food
25. Past tense of 'to be'; I ---
26. Sound a gun makes
27. Jody snapped a dog's nose in one
30. Take back; withdraw
31. ___ Buck; ranch hand
32. Jody asked for only one
36. Easter, for example
38. Jody threw them at birds
39. Nasty; sometimes Jody was ---
40. In a fatherly manner
41. Renown; power to command admiration
43. Bring together
46. Self-satisfied; contented
47. Color of the Pony
49. Carl's old horse
50. He got a pony

DOWN

1. Characteristic of not capable of being upset
2. With a lack of concern; showing indifference
3. Haughty; contemptuous; overbearing
4. Gotten rid of; left out of consideration
5. Explained; interpreted
6. Threateningly
7. Distant; indifferent; apart
8. Equal distance apart at all points; a comparison indicating similarities
11. The red pony resented ____
12. With complexly arranged elements
13. Steadfastness; resoluteness
14. Black ___; the colt
24. Jody's father
28. Prevented action or progress; impeded
29. Energetically; vigorously; actively
33. Jody kills ____ in the haystack
34. Assembled; came together
35. An image that appears only in the mind; ghost
37. Made a low, dull, monotonous sound
40. The Red ___
42. Carry
44. Baby horse
45. Spike on the heel of a cowboy boot
48. Take action

VOCABULARY CROSSWORD - *The Red Pony*

115

VOCABULARY WORKSHEET 1 - *The Red Pony*

_____ 1. Explained; interpreted
    A. Strenuously   B. Construed   C. Ominously   D. Aloof

_____ 2. Steadfastness; resoluteness
    A. Contemplative   B. Vicinity   C. Staunchness   D. Listlessly

_____ 3. Self-satisfied; contented
    A. Martially   B. Imperturbability   C. Complacent   D. Potential

_____ 4. Enraged; angered
    A. Eliminated   B. Imperturbability   C. Incensed   D. Aloof

_____ 5. Belittlingly; reducing in esteem
    A. Disparagingly   B. Languorous   C. Nonchalance   D. Vicinity

_____ 6. Gotten rid of; left out of consideration
    A. Potential   B. Eliminated   C. Listlessly   D. Parallel

_____ 7. With complexly arranged elements
    A. Intricately   B. Perpetually   C. Potential   D. Retract

_____ 8. Indifferently; unenthusiastically
    A. Contemptuously   B. Listlessly   C. Nonchalance   D. Phantom

_____ 9. Latent; possible but not yet so
    A. Martially   B. Parallel   C. Piteously   D. Potential

_____ 10. Continually
    A. Aloof   B. Abruptly   C. Perpetually   D. Retract

_____ 11. Suddenly
    A. Strenuously   B. Perpetually   C. Abruptly   D. Intricately

_____ 12. Renown; power to command admiration
    A. Potential   B. Staunchness   C. Languorous   D. Prestige

_____ 13. Characteristic of not capable of being upset
    A. Eliminated   B. Abruptly   C. Imperturbability   D. Phantom

_____ 14. Energetically; vigorously; actively
    A. Droned   B. Strenuously   C. Disparagingly   D. Whetted

_____ 15. Sorrowfully; dejectedly
    A. Convened   B. Complacent   C. Disconsolately   D. Abruptly

_____ 16. Sharpened
    A. Strenuously   B. Paternally   C. Parallel   D. Whetted

_____ 17. Moving to sympathy
    A. Complacent   B. Staunchness   C. Piteously   D. Retract

_____ 18. Prevented action or progress; impeded
    A. Incensed   B. Arrogant   C. Hampered   D. Retract

_____ 19. With a lack of concern; showing indifference
    A. Nonchalance   B. Disconsolately   C. Convened   D. Prestige

_____ 20. Haughty; contemptuous; overbearing
    A. Arrogant   B. Retract   C. Eliminated   D. Ominously

KEY: VOCABULARY WORKSHEET 1 - *The Red Pony*

_B_ 1. Explained; interpreted
    A. Strenuously   B. Construed   C. Ominously   D. Aloof

_C_ 2. Steadfastness; resoluteness
    A. Contemplative   B. Vicinity   C. Staunchness   D. Listlessly

_C_ 3. Self-satisfied; contented
    A. Martially   B. Imperturbability   C. Complacent   D. Potential

_C_ 4. Enraged; angered
    A. Eliminated   B. Imperturbability   C. Incensed   D. Aloof

_A_ 5. Belittlingly; reducing in esteem
    A. Disparagingly   B. Languorous   C. Nonchalance   D. Vicinity

_B_ 6. Gotten rid of; left out of consideration
    A. Potential   B. Eliminated   C. Listlessly   D. Parallel

_A_ 7. With complexly arranged elements
    A. Intricately   B. Perpetually   C. Potential   D. Retract

_B_ 8. Indifferently; unenthusiastically
    A. Contemptuously   B. Listlessly   C. Nonchalance   D. Phantom

_D_ 9. Latent; possible but not yet so
    A. Martially   B. Parallel   C. Piteously   D. Potential

_C_ 10. Continually
    A. Aloof   B. Abruptly   C. Perpetually   D. Retract

_C_ 11. Suddenly
    A. Strenuously   B. Perpetually   C. Abruptly   D. Intricately

_D_ 12. Renown; power to command admiration
    A. Potential   B. Staunchness   C. Languorous   D. Prestige

_C_ 13. Characteristic of not capable of being upset
    A. Eliminated   B. Abruptly   C. Imperturbability   D. Phantom

_B_ 14. Energetically; vigorously; actively
    A. Droned   B. Strenuously   C. Disparagingly   D. Whetted

_C_ 15. Sorrowfully; dejectedly
    A. Convened   B. Complacent   C. Disconsolately   D. Abruptly

_D_ 16. Sharpened
    A. Strenuously   B. Paternally   C. Parallel   D. Whetted

_C_ 17. Moving to sympathy
    A. Complacent   B. Staunchness   C. Piteously   D. Retract

_C_ 18. Prevented action or progress; impeded
    A. Incensed   B. Arrogant   C. Hampered   D. Retract

_A_ 19. With a lack of concern; showing indifference
    A. Nonchalance   B. Disconsolately   C. Convened   D. Prestige

_A_ 20. Haughty; contemptuous; overbearing
    A. Arrogant   B. Retract   C. Eliminated   D. Ominously

VOCABULARY WORKSHEET 2 - *The Red Pony*

____ 1. PARALLEL   A. Boisterousness; rowdiness

____ 2. PERPETUALLY   B. Threateningly

____ 3. NONCHALANCE   C. Continually

____ 4. RETRACT   D. In a military or warlike manner

____ 5. INCENSED   E. Locality; proximity; neighborhood

____ 6. RAMBUNCTIOUSNESS   F. With complexly arranged elements

____ 7. ALOOF   G. Self-satisfied; contented

____ 8. VICINITY   H. With a lack of concern; showing indifference

____ 9. PHANTOM   I. An image that appears only in the mind; ghost

____ 10. IMPERTURBABILITY J. Sharpened

____ 11. CONSTRUED   K. Equal distance apart at all points; a comparison indicating similarities

____ 12. MARTIALLY   L. Belittlingly; reducing in esteem

____ 13. OMINOUSLY   M. Prevented action or progress; impeded

____ 14. COMPLACENT   N. Distant; indifferent; apart

____ 15. DISPARAGINGLY   O. Characteristic of not capable of being upset

____ 16. PATERNALLY   P. In a fatherly manner

____ 17. WHETTED   Q. Made a low, dull, monotonous sound

____ 18. DRONED   R. Take back; withdraw

____ 19. INTRICATELY   S. Explained; interpreted

____ 20. HAMPERED   T. Enraged; angered

KEY: VOCABULARY WORKSHEET 2 - *The Red Pony*

_K_	1. PARALLEL	A. Boisterousness; rowdiness
_C_	2. PERPETUALLY	B. Threateningly
_H_	3. NONCHALANCE	C. Continually
_R_	4. RETRACT	D. In a military or warlike manner
_T_	5. INCENSED	E. Locality; proximity; neighborhood
_A_	6. RAMBUNCTIOUSNESS	F. With complexly arranged elements
_N_	7. ALOOF	G. Self-satisfied; contented
_E_	8. VICINITY	H. With a lack of concern; showing indifference
_I_	9. PHANTOM	I. An image that appears only in the mind; ghost
_O_	10. IMPERTURBABILITY	J. Sharpened
_S_	11. CONSTRUED	K. Equal distance apart at all points; a comparison indicating similarities
_D_	12. MARTIALLY	L. Belittlingly; reducing in esteem
_B_	13. OMINOUSLY	M. Prevented action or progress; impeded
_G_	14. COMPLACENT	N. Distant; indifferent; apart
_L_	15. DISPARAGINGLY	O. Characteristic of not capable of being upset
_P_	16. PATERNALLY	P. In a fatherly manner
_J_	17. WHETTED	Q. Made a low, dull, monotonous sound
_Q_	18. DRONED	R. Take back; withdraw
_F_	19. INTRICATELY	S. Explained; interpreted
_M_	20. HAMPERED	T. Enraged; angered

VOCABULARY JUGGLE LETTER REVIEW GAME CLUES - *The Red Pony*

SCRAMBLED	WORD	CLUE
PRATUBLY	ABRUPTLY	Suddenly
FOLOA	ALOOF	Distant; indifferent; apart
RAGANORT	ARROGANT	Haughty; contemptuous; overbearing
TCALMEPONC	COMPLACENT	Self-satisfied; contented
RONTESCUD	CONSTRUED	Explained; interpreted
MALOTEVIPCTEN	CONTEMPLATIVE	Thoughtful; meditative
POTESOTUYLUNCM	CONTEMPTUOUSLY	Disdainfully; scornfully
DECNONEV	CONVENED	Assembled; came together
COSAYNODETILLS	DISCONSOLATELY	Sorrowfully; dejectedly
GAGIPYDINLARS	DISPARAGINGLY	Belittlingly; reducing in esteem
NOREDD	DRONED	Made a low, dull, monotonous sound
IMALEDETIN	ELIMINATED	Gotten rid of; left out of consideration
PEAMDREH	HAMPERED	Prevented action or progress; impeded
RPIMBAYLITBERUIT	IMPERTURBABILITY	Characteristic of not capable of being upset
SEEDCINN	INCENSED	Enraged; angered
CLYRINTAETI	INTRICATELY	With complexly arranged elements
GUSNALROOU	LANGUOROUS	Still; sluggish; listless
LETSISLLSY	LISTLESSLY	Indifferently; unenthusiastically
RALTAMIYL	MARTIALLY	In a military or warlike manner
NALOCAHNENC	NONCHALANCE	With a lack of concern; showing indifference
NOOSUYLIM	OMINOUSLY	Threateningly
LAPELRAL	PARALLEL	Equal distance apart at all points; a comparison indicating similarities
TRALPAYENL	PATERNALLY	In a fatherly manner
LUTREYLEPPA	PERPETUALLY	Continually
PHATOMN	PHANTOM	An image that appears only in the mind; ghost
SEPUYOITL	PITEOUSLY	Moving to sympathy
PLATONTIE	POTENTIAL	Latent; possible but not yet so
SRIPETEG	PRESTIGE	Renown; power to command admiration
NAMOUSESCTUBRINS	RAMBUNCTIOUSNESS	Boisterousness; rowdiness
CARTERT	RETRACT	Take back; withdraw
TUNHESNSCAS	STAUNCHNESS	Steadfastness; resoluteness